Epistemology

ROYAL INSTITUTE OF PHILOSOPHY SUPPLEMENT: 64

EDITED BY

Anthony O'Hear

CAMBRIDGE
UNIVERSITY PRESS

PUBLISHED BY THE PRESS SYNDICATE OF THE UNIVERSITY OF CAMBRIDGE
The Pitt Building, Trumpington Street, Cambridge, CB2 1RP,
United Kingdom

CAMBRIDGE UNIVERSITY PRESS
The Edinburgh Building, Cambridge CB2 8RU, United Kingdom
32 Avenue of the Americas, New York, NY 10013–2473, USA
477 Williamstown Road, Port Melbourne, VIC 3207, Australia
Ruiz de Alarcón 13, 28014 Madrid, Spain
Dock House, The Waterfront, Cape Town 8001, South Africa

Printed in the United Kingdom at the University Press, Cambridge
Typeset by Techset Composition Ltd, Salisbury, UK

A catalogue record for this book is available from the British Library

Library of Congress Cataloguing-in-Publication Data applied for

ISBN 9780521138581
ISSN 1358-2461

Contents

Preface   v

Notes on Contributors   vii

Social Epistemology: Theory and Applications   1
ALVIN I. GOLDMAN

Knowledge, Understanding and Epistemic Value   19
DUNCAN PRITCHARD

Knowledge of Counterfactuals   45
TIMOTHY WILLIAMSON

How I Know I'm Not a Brain in a Vat   65
JOSÉ L. ZALABARDO

Belief, Reason & Logic   89
SCOTT STURGEON

What is Knowledge?   101
QUASSIM CASSAM

The Value of Knowledge and The Test of Time   121
MIRANDA FRICKER

Index of Names   139

Preface

This volume is based on lectures given as the Royal Institute of Philosophy's annual lecture series, held in London during the autumn and spring terms of 2006–7.

At least since the 17th century Epistemology has played a role in philosophy. While its foundational status has come to be questioned its overall importance has not. The papers in this volume give a good indication of current directions in the field, from some of those whose contributions are at the forefront of epistemological enquiry.

I would like to thank the contributors, both for their lectures and for their contributions to this volume. Adam Ferner prepared the index and did much of the editorial work, and I would like to express my gratitude to him too.

Anthony O'Hear

Notes on Contributors

Alvin I. Goldman
> Alvin I. Goldman is Professor of Philosophy and Cognitive Science at Rutgers, The State University of New Jersey.

Duncan Pritchard
> Duncan Pritchard holds the Chair in Epistemology at the University of Edinburgh.

Timothy Williamson
> Timothy Williamson is the Wykeham Professor of Logic at the University of Oxford.

José L. Zalabardo
> José L. Zalabardo is Reader at University College London.

Scott Sturgeon
> Scott Sturgeon is CUF lecturer at Wadham College, Oxford.

Quassim Cassam
> Quassim Cassam is professor of Philosophy at Warwick University.

Miranda Fricker
> Miranda Fricker is Reader in the School of Philosophy at Birkbeck, University of London.

Social Epistemology: Theory and Applications

ALVIN I. GOLDMAN

1. Mainstream Epistemology and Social Epistemology

Epistemology has had a strongly individualist orientation, at least since Descartes. Knowledge, for Descartes, starts with the fact of one's own thinking and with oneself as subject of that thinking. Whatever else can be known, it must be known by inference from one's own mental contents. Achieving such knowledge is an individual, rather than a collective, enterprise. Descartes's successors largely followed this lead, so the history of epistemology, down to our own time, has been a predominantly individualist affair.

There are scattered exceptions. A handful of historical epistemologists gave brief space to the question of knowing, or believing justifiably, based on the testimony of others. Testimony-based knowledge would be one step into a more social epistemology. Hume took it for granted that we regularly rely on the factual statements of others, and argued that it is reasonable to do so if we have adequate reasons for trusting the veracity of these sources. However, reasons for such trust, according to Hume, must rest on personal observations of people's veracity or reliability.[1] Thomas Reid took a different view. He claimed that our natural attitude of trusting others is reasonable even if we know little if anything about others' reliability. Testimony, at least sincere testimony, is always *prima facie* credible (Reid 1970: 240–241). Here we have two philosophers of the 18th century both endorsing at least one element of what nowadays is called "social epistemology." But these points did not much occupy either Hume's or Reid's corpus of philosophical writing; nor were

---

[1] Hume wrote: "[T]here is no species of reasoning more common, more useful, and even necessary to human life, than that which is derived from the testimony of men, and the reports of eye-witnesses and spectators... [O]ur assurance in any argument of this kind is derived from no other principle than our observation of the veracity of human testimony, and of the usual conformity of facts to the reports of witnesses." (Hume 1972: 11)

doi:10.1017/S1358246109000022

Alvin I. Goldman

these passages much studied or cited by their contemporaries and immediate successors.

Fast forward now to the second half of the 20th century. Here we find intellectual currents pointing toward the socializing of epistemology. Several of these movements, however, were centered outside of philosophy and never adopted the label of "social epistemology," or adopted it only belatedly. I have in mind movements in the social studies of science and cultural studies. In science studies, the most influential figure was Thomas Kuhn, whose *Structure of Scientific Revolutions* (1962) was itself a revolution in the interpretation of science. Kuhn influenced other investigators in the history and sociology of science to view science as just another social institution, not as a paragon of objective rationality, the stance that had been standard among positivist philosophers of science. According to Kuhn, the replacement of one scientific paradigm by a rival does not occur because the old paradigm is rationally overwhelmed by new evidence. Rival paradigms, according to Kuhn, aren't even (evidentially) "commensurable". It appeared, in other words, that Kuhn denied any rational basis for scientific revolution. Instead, it has a social basis. Although Kuhn's precise commitments were ambiguous, many thought that, according to Kuhn, paradigm change is just a matter of "mob psychology" (Lakatos 1970: 178). In the wake of Kuhn, many historians and sociologists of science abandoned a rational perspective on science in favor of a sociological one. An earlier champion of this idea was Ludwig Fleck (1979).

Kuhn also expressed doubt about *truth* as the goal of science, or at least as an achievable goal, and other sociologists of science followed suit. Thus, in the 1970s, the "strong programme" in the sociology of science emerged, centered in Edinburgh, that sought to study science without any assumption that science uses methods that are either rational or superior avenues to truth. Indeed, along with postmodern thinkers like Michel Foucault, many of these authors contended that so-called scientific "facts" or "truths" are mere *social constructions*. What happens in scientific laboratories isn't the discovery of scientific truths, but their creation or "fabrication." Latour and Woolgar wrote:

> [W]e do not conceive of scientists ... as pulling back the curtain on pregiven, but hitherto concealed truths. Rather, objects are constituted through the artful creativity of scientists. (1986: 128–129)

So-called truth, facts, rationality – they are all a matter, not of mind-independent, or society-independent nature, but of social negotiation or politics.

2

Social Epistemology: Theory and Applications

Most writers in sociology of science have shied away from calling their enterprise "social epistemology," but this *is* the label chosen by Steve Fuller, both for the title of his first book (1988) and for a journal he founded. Is this an apt label for this group of ideas? Well, what is epistemology? It is typically defined as the *theory of knowledge*. This invites the question: What is knowledge? Mainstream epistemologists universally agree that knowledge implies truth, that knowledge is factive. If your belief isn't true, it isn't a piece of knowledge. Social constructivists, though they talk about knowledge, are characteristically dismissive or disparaging of truth. There are no facts, they maintain, only what is believed by this or that individual or community. For social constructivists, then, knowledge is simply what is believed, or at least what is communally believed.

In my book on social epistemology, *Knowledge in a Social World* (1999) I introduced a term to describe postmodernists and social constructivists of the foregoing persuasion. I called them *veriphobes*, because they display an aversion or abhorrence of truth. (The prefix 'veri' in 'veriphobe' is derived from the Latin 'veritas'.) The affliction from which they suffer is called *veriphobia*. Let me now introduce an obvious antonym of 'veriphobia,' viz. *veriphilia*. Mainstream epistemologists are lovers of truth; at least they are comfortable doing epistemology with the truth concept in hand. No doubt there are many philosophical problems concerning truth, both logical and metaphysical. Still, traditional epistemologists (of the last 50–60 years) help themselves to the assumption that some propositions are true, others are false, and what makes them true or false are (generally) mind-independent and community-independent facts, which we may call "truth-makers." The exact nature of truth-makers is controversial, but their characteristic independence of human construction or fabrication is taken as given.

2. Veriphobic Social Epistemology

What would social epistemology consist in under the aegis of veriphobia and veriphilia respectively? Veriphobes, at least those within the social studies of science camp, are usually interested in explanation. They want to provide social explanations, whether historical or sociological, of various knowledge-related episodes in social life, especially in science. These are knowledge-related episodes under *their* construal of 'knowledge,' which, as explained above, comes to little more than *belief*, or *collective belief*. The proposed

3

explanations would deliberately make no reference to any truth-values of the beliefs in question. This was a core tenet of the strong programme, as championed by Barry Barnes and David Bloor (1982). They enunciated the "symmetry" principle, under which the same types of causes would explain both true and false beliefs, both rational and irrational beliefs.

Is a sociology of science that totally rejects truth really feasible? Do veriphobes consistently adhere to such a project? No. An *explanation* of any phenomenon – a genuine explanation, rather than a merely putative one – must invoke events and processes that *truly* occurred, and if it's a causal explanation, it must be *true* that those events and processes had a causal influence on the phenomenon to be explained. This is tacitly appreciated by the relatively careful scientific work that social constructivists conduct. They do minute observations of laboratory life in all (or many) of its details. They do careful historical work to unearth the causal factors that contributed to this or that episode in the history of science. What makes sense of all this diligent effort if not the goal of getting the story right, of telling it as it was, i.e. of getting the *truth*? So, pervasive rejection of truth cannot co-exist with their own scientific projects.

Here is a second familiar problem with the veriphobic rejection of truth or factuality. Fact-constructivism runs into the obvious problem that the world did not begin with us humans. The Big Bang and the formation of the Earth occurred before we were around. So how could *we* have constructed them? Bruno Latour was ready to bite the bullet on this question, at least on one occasion. When French sociologists working on the mummy of Ramses II, who died in 1213 BC, concluded that Ramses probably died of tuberculosis, Latour denied that this was possible. "How could he pass away due to a bacillus discovered by Robert Koch in 1881?" As Latour boldly put it, "Before Koch, the bacillus had no real existence."[2]

If, as social constructivists say, a bacillus comes into existence when the scientific community comes to believe in its existence, how is a case to be handled in which scientists come to believe in a bacillus (or other scientific posit) and later abandon this belief? Did the bacillus exist for a while and then cease to exist? Or was its existence permanently assured because *at one time* the scientific community believed in it? What about multiple scientific communities taking different stances on the question? Does the consensus of a single community trump the counter-consensus of a second? Or do we have to

---

[2]   See Boghossian 2006: 26, who cites a quotation of Latour by Alan Sokal and Jean Bricment 1998: 96–97.

count numbers of scientists? Under the latter scenario, if 273 bio-chemists accept the existence of a certain bacillus and 271 are skeptical, then it exists. And what if five biochemists lost in the woods and presumed dead are now found to have survived, and all reject the bacillus? Does this imply that it never existed in the first place? These are among the conundrums that descend upon us if we adopt the crazy position of fact-constructivism.

Rather less bizarre is a somewhat analogous view about rationality or justification. Social constructivists are equally concerned to dispute the objectivity of these notions. Suppose that two people – say Galileo and Cardinal Bellarmine, his Vatican prosecutor – disagree about whether the earth circles the sun. Each claims to be justified in his belief and denies that the other is so justified. Presumably, if they were pressed to spell out the detailed basis of their justification, each might spell out a system of epistemic principles, or rules of belief justification, that countenance the present belief as justified. Although the two systems might overlap in some of their principles, there would undoubtedly be differences among them. Galileo's system would license belief in astronomical matters based on what one sees when one looks through a telescope. It might deny the evidential relevance to astronomy of what is found in Holy Scripture. Cardinal Bellarmine's system would feature opposing principles, principles that endorse the evidential relevance (indeed, decisiveness) of Holy Scripture and dispute the evidential relevance of telescopic observation to the properties of heavenly bodies. So, which system of epistemic principles, or rules of justification, is correct? More fundamentally, is there a matter of correctness, or more or less correctness, in the matter of epistemic systems? Are there facts of justification independent of what individuals or communities say or think? This is a serious question for epistemology.

This problem of objective rationality or justifiedness is pressed by Richard Rorty (1979). Rorty holds that there is no "objective" basis for adopting one system, or set of epistemic standards, rather than another (1979: 331). Galileo *created* the notion of "scientific values," or standards, but the question of whether he was (objectively) "rational" in doing so is out of place (1979: 331). Paul Boghossian (2006) spells out Rorty's position in order to criticize it. Construing Rorty as an epistemic relativist, he spells out the relativist thesis, offers an argument on behalf of the relativist, and then critiques the position. The linchpin of the argument is that there is no way for either Galileo or Cardinal Bellarmine to justify the acceptance of their respective epistemic systems. If either of those epistemic systems were objectively right, it should be possible to justify a

Alvin I. Goldman

belief in its rightness. Why can't a belief in its rightness be justified? Because, argues the relativist (as Boghossian presents him), any justification would have to rest on an epistemic system, presumably the *same* system that the protagonist begins with. But to defend a system by appeal to itself is *circular*, and hence illegitimate. According to the relativist, then, no such justification can be provided, and no such objective (or "absolute") fact of justification obtains.

How successful is this argument for justificational relativism? Boghossian offers several lines of criticism, which are too complex to pursue here. I'll offer a different line of criticism. The relativist's argument against the possibility of justifying one's own epistemic system rests on the charge that it involves a kind of circularity – not "premise circularity," in the language of epistemologists, but "epistemic circularity" – plus the assumption that this kind of circularity is a *bad* or *illegitimate* thing. Epistemic circularity can be illustrated in connection with inductive inference. Suppose someone asks you to justify induction by showing that it is generally reliable, i.e. it generally leads to true conclusions. You reply, "Well, I used induction on occasion O_1 and it led to a true conclusion; I used induction on occasion O_2 and it again led to a true conclusion; and so forth. Therefore [conclusion], induction generally leads to true conclusions [to be interpreted as referring to past, present and future]." This attempted justification *uses* induction to justify induction. That's an instance of epistemic circularity, which is a bad thing according to this relativist argument. What kind of "bad thing" is it, allegedly? Presumably, it's bad as a tool of justification. If this is right, the relativist is assuming that there is some *fact of the matter* about the illegitimacy of certain patterns of inference. The relativist isn't entitled, however, to appeal to any such justificational fact. Objective facts in matters of justification are precisely what the relativist is denying! So relativism about justificational facts is difficult to sustain and hasn't yet been done successfully. I won't pursue further forays into this territory.

3. Veriphiliac Social Epistemology

By my lights, justification and rationality are trickier topics than truth. So the style of objectivist social epistemology I have tried to develop (especially in *Knowledge in a Social World*) emphasizes truth over justification and rationality. I'll continue this emphasis here, without for a moment denying that justification and rationality (including group rationality) are important and legitimate topics for the field.

It is commonplace among (mainstream) epistemologists to say that our twin intellectual goals are to obtain true belief and avoid false belief (error). Instead of talking of "goals," one can talk of "values." One might say that it is more valuable, from an intellectual point of view, to have a true belief on some selected question than to have a false belief. If the question is whether P or not-P is the case, and the truth of the matter is P, then it's better to believe P than to believe not-P. Another stance one might take on the question of P versus not-P is agnosticism, indecision, or withholding of judgment. On the standard line, such an attitude would be of intermediate value between believing a truth (P, in this case) and believing a falsehood (not-P, in this case). If there are such attitudes as "degrees of belief" (or degrees of confidence), we could extend these ideas and say that believing P to degree .90 has more value than believing P to degree .70. Thus, we have a ranking of possible attitudes toward a truth, such that the highest degree of belief toward the truth (1.0, full belief) has the greatest value, and every weaker degree of belief toward the same truth has a lesser value (perhaps negative, beyond a certain point).

What kind of value is this? In *Knowledge in a Social World* I called it *veritistic value*. 'Veritistic' connotes truth-centeredness, as opposed to a concern with justification or rationality. The latter epistemic notions express one or more different kinds of epistemic value, where the precise connections to veritistic value are controversial. In KSW, and in the remainder of my remarks here, I focus on veritistic value, or notions closely affiliated with it.

How does veritistic value link up with *social* epistemology? There is nothing social about a single agent having a true or false belief. Fair enough; but a wide variety of social practices and institution can have causal impacts, often immense causal influences, on the attitudes of individuals, tilting them either toward true beliefs or toward false ones. Large sectors of social interchange involve the transmission of communications – often embodying information, misinformation, partial information. The practices of communication that take place in these social networks can be studied from the vantage point of their impact on the veritistic-value states of multiple individuals. This is how I conceive of social epistemology, at least *veritistic* social epistemology.[3]

---

[3] There is a clear parallel between the social "practices" of veritistic social epistemology and the cognitive "processes" that play a pivotal role in the reliabilist form of individual epistemology I have advocated. (See especially Goldman 1979, 1986.)

Alvin I. Goldman

"Sectors" of society might be divided into the (relatively) *private* and the (relatively) *public*. Perhaps these can be arranged on a continuum. At one end is the purely private sector, featuring conversational practices in which individuals convey their beliefs to other individuals ('testimony') or engage in argumentation to persuade others of their views. At the other end of the continuum are highly regulated public practices, for example, the carefully structured proceedings of a courtroom, where a judge oversees the speech of attorneys and witnesses, and controls the items of purported evidence that are admitted into court. Somewhere between the ends of the continuum are the communications that occur in various electronic platforms. Some facilitate individual-to-individual communication that differs little from face-to-face communication. Other electronic platforms feature more in the way of "supervisors" or "gatekeepers" of communication. Other media, ranging from conventional newspapers to weblogs, fall somewhere along the continuum. All of these sectors involve "social" practices, in an inclusive sense of the term.

In the rest of this paper I'll concentrate on what can reasonably be considered "institutions" involving communication. In each such institution, there are indefinitely many possible ways to structure them, indefinitely many rules or procedures that might govern communicative exchange. Veritistic social epistemology is interested in how to design rules or procedures that improve veritistic outcomes. Like traditional epistemology generally, it is a normative enterprise, not a purely descriptive or explanatory one, although it may require layers of descriptive materials on which to base its normative recommendations.

4. Laws of Speech and Legal Adjudication

Ordinary statutes, constitutional provisions, common-law practices, and judicial interpretations are obvious examples of institutions that can produce better or worse veritistic outcomes. Some statutes, judicial interpretations, etc. either constitute or have definite bearings on government policies of speech and the press. One such example is a ruling by Britain's highest court, the Law Lords, concerning British libel law (New York Times, October 12, 2006). Under British libel law, newspapers being sued are required to prove the truth of the allegations they print – the opposite of the situation in the United States, where the burden of proof falls heavily on plaintiffs. According to many authorities, until now the odds of journalists' winning libel cases have been stacked against them. In the recent case that prompted the high court's ruling, the European edition of the Wall Street Journal reported that Saudi Arabia was monitoring bank accounts of prominent Saudi businesses and individuals to trace whether they were being used, possibly unwittingly, to siphon money to terrorist groups. One of the businesses sued the newspaper. The newspaper could not prove the truth of their allegations because, in the nature of things, the existence of surveillance by highly secretive Saudi authorities would have been impossible to prove by evidence in open court. Still, the paper argued that the article was in the public interest. The Law Lords agreed with this contention. One member of the panel wrote: "It is no part of the duty of the press to cooperate with any government ... in order to keep from the public information of public interest ...". Several commentators agreed that this decision should make it easier for newspapers in the U.K. to publish serious stories where they cannot prove that allegations are true, as long as articles are responsibly reported, including the use of confidential sources.

What will be the veritistic outcomes of this change in judicial policy? Before the policy change, so it is argued, stories were not being printed – presumably true stories – because of constant fear of lawsuits. Even people from abroad sued in English courts because English judges were so sympathetic to libel plaintiffs. The judges were presumably motivated to prevent false and defamatory stories from being printed, thereby generating false beliefs. But the result of favoring libel plaintiffs was to impede the publication of true stories (in the public interest). The change in policy, therefore, will arguably have positive veritistic consequences on balance.

The veritistic analysis of legal adjudication systems focuses on a particular division of a legal system, the division responsible for determining guilt or innocence, liability or non-liability, of defendants. I shall assume that, when the law is sufficiently precise, and the true facts of the case fall determinately on one side or other of the law, then each charge brought against a defendant is either true or false. Finally, I assume (for a defense, see *Knowledge in a Social World*) that the principal aim of the adjudication arm of the law is to reach accurate verdicts on the charges, given the law and the genuine facts of the case. For any given adjudication system, then, we can ask how well it succeeds in this veritistic task. How frequently does it generate truths rather than falsehoods with respect to guilt or innocence, liability or non-liability? We can also ask comparative questions of the same sort. How reliable is one style of system as compared to a different style of system, e.g. the adversary system of the Anglo-American tradition as compared with the so-called "inquisitorial" system (a very bad label, of course) of the Continental tradition? Getting more specific, we can ask how well some present version of the Anglo-American system works as compared to a version that would result if we tweaked its rules in various ways, for example, by changing the jury-selection procedure, or the instructions that judges give to jurors, or by changing some rule of evidence. All this could be asked in the spirit of contemplating actual institutional changes.

5. Problems with Forensic Laboratories: A Model Case of Veritistic Social Epistemology

Another institution whose proper function is to (help) obtain the truth is forensic science. Unfortunately, several academic treatments indicate that this function is not being well served by current practice. Saks et al. (2001) report that erroneous and fraudulent expert evidence from forensic scientists is one of the major causes, perhaps the leading cause, of erroneous convictions of innocent persons. One rogue scientist engaged in rampant falsification for 15 years, and another faked more than 100 autopsies and falsified dozens of toxicology and blood reports (Kelly and Wearne 1998; Koppl 2006). Shocking cases are found in more than one country.

Can the error rate from forensic laboratory reports be reduced? This is a question of institutional (re-)design discussed by an economist, Roger Koppl, who offers a theoretical analysis and an experimental finding that supports this analysis. Finally, he offers a particular suggestion for improving the veritistic properties of the current system.

Koppl (2006) pinpoints the problem as the monopoly position enjoyed by most forensic laboratories vis-à-vis the legal jurisdictions that hire them. Each jurisdiction is served by one lab, and only that lab delivers reports about crime scene evidence. A typical report says whether or not there's a match between an evidentiary item from the crime scene and a trait of the defendant, e.g. a match between a DNA sample found at the crime scene and the DNA profile of the defendant. Knowing that prosecutors prefer messages reporting a match, forensic workers have a bias toward reporting matches. Koppl analyzes the situation by means of game-theoretic models of epistemic systems. Each model contains one or more senders who search a message space and deliver a message to one or more receivers. In forensic science the receivers are jurors who hear the message delivered via testimony in open court.

The jury then decides whether a fingerprint or some DNA sample left at the crime scene belongs to the defendant. This is one input into the jury's deliberation that culminates in a judgment of guilt or innocence.

On the basis of a game-theoretic analysis, Koppl argues that in the absence of competition with any other forensic lab, the bias toward reporting matches will produce a high incidence of false information. If competition were introduced into the institutional arrangement, however, e.g. by having three forensic labs produce reports, this competition would create new incentives, more unfavorable to the transmission of false information. Koppl and colleagues performed a gaming experiment designed to mimic the scenarios for forensic laboratories. This experiment confirmed a change in behavior in the predicted direction. The three-sender situation reduced the systemic error rate by two-thirds (as compared with the one-sender situation). This is a fine example of what Koppl calls "epistemic systems design," where we study the impact of system re-design on matters of veracity. It contrasts with the standard question in economics that focuses on the *efficiency* of institutional systems.

6. When Ignorance is Desirable: A Broadened Conception of Veriphiliac Social Epistemology

I have discussed veritistic value in terms of a specific ordering of doxastic attitudes directed at a true proposition. According to this order, higher strengths of belief in a true proposition always confer greater veritistic value with respect to that proposition (or the question that it answers). In different terminology, a state of being informed that P is veritistically preferable to being uninformed that P (e.g. with-holding judgment on P), which is veritistically preferable to being misinformed that P (believing P where it's false).

Our illustrations make it clear that many social institutions have as part of their goal or function to promote veritistically good states among occupants of certain institutional roles (with respect to selected questions). For example, legal proceedings have the goal of promoting veritistically good states in the fact-finder with respect to questions of guilt versus innocence. But not all institutions have such a goal. In fact, there are cases in which an institution ought to promote veritistically *bad* states in certain individuals or role-players. Being informed is not always better than being uninformed or misinformed, at least for some people in some social settings (and sometimes in purely individual settings).

11

What are some examples? One type of case arises from the desirability of *privacy*. It is generally conceded that people have rights or legitimate interests in keeping certain facts about themselves private, which means keeping other people ignorant of those facts. The relevant facts include their social security number, their cash machine PIN, their medical records, what they do in their bedroom, and so forth. If society ought to protect person X's privacy with respect to fact F, then society should take steps to ensure that quite a few people other than X – most people, in fact – are ignorant of F.

A more novel example involves elections and democratic institutions. The United States Supreme Court, in the name of the First Amendment, has struck down efforts to restrict overall spending on election campaigns. The idea is that voters have a right to vote for their favored candidates not only by casting a ballot in the voting booth but also by supporting those candidates' electoral campaigns with dollars. The result, of course, is the corruption that ensues when elected officials "pay off" those interest groups who donated lots of money. Government is bought by the highest bidders. Of course, politicians cannot deliver the goods to their campaign contributors in so obvious a fashion. But there are plenty of opportunities to deliver in more subtle, or deniable, ways.

What is to be done? One solution on which both liberal and conservative reformers have converged is the "full information" idea. Candidates are required to reveal who is bankrolling their campaigns, and how much they are giving. If knowledge of the bankrollers is shared with the public, the latter will theoretically be in a position to be watchdogs on the winning candidates' conduct in office.

There is also a much less well-known idea, but (by my lights) more promising. Why not require campaign contributions to be *anonymous?* That way, with candidates not knowing who gave them a lot of money, they won't be in a position to reward the contributors. This has been proposed by Bruce Ackerman and Ian Ayres (2002). Historically, Ackerman and Ayres point out, the secret ballot came to America only during the late nineteenth century. Previously voters cast their ballots in full view of the contesting parties, who carefully monitored each decision. Within this framework, corrupt vote buying was commonplace. The situation was transformed by the secret ballot. Once a voter could promise to vote one way and actually vote another, it wasn't easy for him to sell his vote, because vote-buyers could no longer verify the credibility of a voter's commitment. Suddenly, a voter's promise to sell his vote for money became worthless.

Social Epistemology: Theory and Applications

Ackerman and Ayres use the same logic in dealing with campaign contributions. They propose the "secret donation booth". Contributors will be barred from giving money directly to candidates. Instead they must pass their checks through a blind trust. Candidates would get access to the money deposited in their account with the blind trust, but won't be able to identify who provided the funds. Many people will, of course, claim to have contributed vast sums, but none of them will be able to prove it. Just as the secret voting booth disrupts vote buying because candidates are uncertain how a citizen actually voted, anonymous donations would disrupt influence peddling because candidates would be uncertain whether givers actually gave what they say they gave.

There are many details that would have to be handled to make the anonymity process work. Ackerman and Ayres haven't sold their proposal widely as of yet; to my knowledge, it hasn't reached the threshold of public discussion. For the sake of argument, however, suppose it's a good idea that would really work. It is then a case in which ignorance by certain people, viz. political candidates, of certain facts about others, viz. who has contributed to their campaigns and who hasn't, is an institutional desideratum. If Ackerman and Ayres are right, it is preferable from the perspective of democratic institutions that certain crucial role players, viz. candidates for office, have veritistically inferior, not superior, positions vis-à-vis certain propositions.

How is this relevant to social epistemology? A veritistic social epistemologist might reply as follows: "Such cases should be of no interest to us, because these are cases where veritistic desiderata don't kick in. So we should simply ignore such cases." But there's another possible response, involving a non-trivial re-design of the foundations of social epistemology.

Let us abandon the assumption that social epistemology (SE) should evaluate all outcomes of interest in terms of the outcome ranking discussed earlier. Under that old style of outcome ranking, true belief is always superior to withholding of judgment, for any given proposition. This ranking style is firmly tied to the notion of "veritistic value". We now propose, however, that SE not be wedded to veritistic value. V-value could remain central to SE, just not essential to it. In some institutional contexts, we might allow, it is desirable to advocate a different informational policy, one that cuts against true belief as the best condition for all parties, one that views ignorance as preferable to knowledge for some individuals. At least this would be the preferable ranking from a social or institutional perspective. This wouldn't imply that the individuals

Alvin I. Goldman

themselves would prefer ignorance to being informed (on the matters in question).[4]

Is this a tenable proposal for a conception of SE? What would then distinguish SE from other parts of social philosophy or social theory? Wouldn't the contemplated change divest the enterprise of its distinctively epistemological dimension? What would it have in common with epistemology as usually conceived? Isn't a preference for truth over error or ignorance just built into the conception of the epistemic?

What is still distinctive to SE is the focus on what I'll call "veridoxic" states as the states of interest. A veridoxic state is a state with two components. The first component is a doxastic attitude, like belief, disbelief, and withholding of judgment. The second component is a truth value: either truth or falsity. So, each of the states described earlier in our V-value scheme are veridoxic states. Under the new proposal, SE would continue to focus on this class of states. The difference is that the new proposal would no longer have us restrict attention to the "canonical" ranking of veridoxic states associated with veritism. It would not cling to the treatment of true belief as being superior to false belief or withholding, from a social point of view (or even from an individual point of view). We could distinguish this canonical ranking from alternative rankings, where the latter rankings also concern veridoxic states. By contrast with social constructivists and other fact-relativists, we would insist that the propositional contents of doxastic states are (typically) either true or false. We would not insist, however, that SE take a purely truth preferring (i.e. true-belief preferring) stance for all agents and all societal topics. The desirability of privacy is a sign that no such stance is warranted. Numerous other examples are readily produced. In time of war (just war, at any rate), it isn't incumbent on a society to deliver military secrets to the enemy. It's entirely legitimate to retain its secrets despite the fact that successful secrecy entails ignorance on the part of others.

I can already hear the predictable complaints of my epistemologist colleagues: "OK, it isn't good from the society's viewpoint to deliver its military secrets to the enemy. And if that society's cause is just, delivering military secrets to the enemy isn't good from the standpoint of justice. Nonetheless, it's good *from an epistemic point of view* to do so. Transmission of truths is always epistemically good, at least truths of interest to the hearers or recipients. That's just the distinctive nature of epistemology and the epistemic."

---

[4] Sometimes even individuals have reasons to prefer ignorance to knowledge. See the case described in note 5 below.

14

What shall we say, then, about the following two cases, where veritistic ends demand "anti-veritistic" means? Take Koppl's example of forensic laboratories and their relationships to courts. If Koppl's proposal were adopted of hiring multiple forensic laboratories to report on the same items of evidence, it could be that it would deter biased reporting for each laboratory to be ignorant of what the other laboratories report. Only such ignorance can guarantee that the laboratories not be complicit with one another. Notice, however, that this ignorance is a means to achieve an ultimate state of accurate judgment on the part of the fact-finder (the jury). So we cannot say that our interest in the laboratories' being ignorant of one another's reports is not of *social epistemological* interest, because we certainly want to regard the forensic laboratory case as a specimen problem for social epistemology.

Similarly, consider the desirability of journalists maintaining the confidentiality of their sources. To maintain confidentiality is to keep the public ignorant of who these sources are. Could that possibly be a socially good informational state? Certainly, it could be (and probably is, in many cases). Moreover, it is socially good because of the larger informational payoffs. If a source would decline to disclose publicly important information to a reporter unless his identity is kept confidential, then the public wouldn't receive the information in question. Surely the whole field of public information policy deserves to be treated under the heading of social epistemology. If keeping sources' identities secret is an epistemically illicit act – from the "get-go", as it were – the social epistemology of this subject will be unacceptably constrained or circumscribed.

Again, the response of (some) other epistemologists is predictable. "We should distinguish *intrinsic* versus *instrumental* epistemic value. A state of affairs is intrinsically valuable from an epistemic point of view only if it has (positive) veritistic value, where true belief is superior to ignorance, for example. But this doesn't preclude the possibility that a state of affairs have instrumentally (positive) epistemic value even by being a state of ignorance rather than true belief. That's still of interest to social epistemology, so long as the final end which the ignorance promotes is a veritistically good state such as knowledge or true belief."

This is one route that social epistemology might take. But it doesn't strike me as the best route, certainly not a required route. Notice that the sought-after states of knowledge (true belief) in the two cases just cited – the forensic laboratories case and the confidential sources case – are not sought after purely for their own sake. In each case, there is a plausible further end beyond the sought-after veritistic states. In the forensic laboratories case, it is delivering justice with respect to the criminal matters before the court. Justice is the final end, and accurate judgment by the jury is a means to that end. Similarly, the reason one wants vital information reported to the public is so they can *act* in the public's interest. The sought-after knowledge states are themselves not "final," intrinsic ends. So it doesn't seem reasonable to admit these cases into the sphere of social epistemology while excluding the campaign-donation anonymity proposal.

Let me try to clarify this proposal for a modified conception of social epistemology by drawing an analogy with engineering. The science (or art) of engineering isn't responsible for the aims that various users might wish to achieve for a sought-after object or system to be engineered. Most people who want a bridge to be built would want the bridge to be very strong and capable of withstanding as much weight as possible (relative to cost constraints). But there might be exceptions. A small country surrounded by aggressive and highly armed neighbors might prefer to have weak rather than strong bridges built over the rivers that constitute their borders. This might be seen as a means to keep invading tanks from getting across the bridges. Weak bridges would conveniently collapse under the weight of tanks. It would be a good engineering feat to have bridges designed to withstand the weight of ordinary commercial traffic but not tank traffic. In general, engineering deals with the design and production of artifacts that meet specifications independently arrived at. Engineering per se doesn't fix the desired specifications. Similarly, SE would not try to fix the specifications for desirable veridoxic states. For some purposes, ignorance (on the part of some) might be better than knowledge. SE is prepared to work with all sorts of ranking specifications. But it aims to figure out the social practices and institutional arrangements that promote higher attainments on whatever veridoxic rankings are appropriate, using normative considerations independent of SE per se.[5]

Rutgers, The State University of New Jersey

[5]   Notice that similar considerations apply to purely *individual* choice situations. There are cases in which an individual might prefer being ignorant to being knowledgeable, even when no "social" desiderata are in play. For example, one might prefer to be ignorant of any intended messages that a potential blackmailer might send him. If the agent doesn't receive or learn of the blackmailer's message, he can't really be blackmailed (at least if the potential blackmailer knows that the agent is ignorant). Thanks to Holly Smith for this point and (Thomas Schelling's) example.

References

Ackerman, Bruce and Ayres, Ian (2002) *Voting with Dollars: A New Paradigm for Campaign Finance*. New Haven, Yale University Press.

Boghossian, Paul (2006) *Fear of Knowledge*. New York, Oxford University Press.

Barnes, Barry and Bloor, David (1982) "Relativism, Rationalism and the Sociology of Knowledge," in *Rationality and Relativism* (eds.) M. Hollis and S. Lukes. Cambridge, Mass: MIT Press.

Fleck, Ludwig (1979) *The Genesis and Development of a Scientific Fact*, (eds.) T. J. Trenn and R. K. Merton. Chicago, Ill, University of Chicago Press.

Fuller, Steve (1988) *Social Epistemology*. Bloomington, Ind, Indiana University Press.

Goldman, Alvin (1979) "What Is Justified Belief," in *Justification and Knowledge*, (ed.) G. Pappas. Dordrecht, Reidel. Reprinted in Goldman, *Liaisons: Philosophy Meets the Cognitive and Social Sciences*. Cambridge, Mass, MIT Press.

————— (1986) *Epistemology and Cognition*. Cambridge, Mass, Harvard University Press.

————— (1999) *Knowledge in a Social World*. Oxford, Oxford University Press.

Hume, David (1972) *Enquiries Concerning Human Understanding and Concerning the Principles of Morals* (1977), (ed.) L. A. Selby-Bigge, 2nd edn. Oxford, Oxford University Press.

Kelly, J. F. and Wearne, P. (1998) *Tainting Evidence: Inside the Scandals at the FBI Crime Lab*. New York, Free Press.

Koppl, Roger (2006) "Democratic Epistemics: An Experiment on How to Improve Forensic Science." http://papers.econ.mpg.de/evo/discussionpapers/2006-09.pdf

Kuhn, Thomas (1962) *The Structure of Scientific Revolutions*. Chicago, Ill, University of Chicago Press.

Lakatos, Imre (1970) "Falsification and the Methodology of Scientific Research Programmes," in *Criticism and the Growth of Knowledge* (91–196), (eds.) I. Lakatos and A. Musgrave. Cambridge, Cambridge University Press.

Latour, Bruno and Woolgar, Steve (1986) *Laboratory Life: The Construction of Scientific Facts*. Princeton, NJ, Princeton University Press.

Reid, Thomas (1970) *An Inquiry into the Human Mind*, ed. Timothy Duggan. Chicago, Ill, University of Chicago Press.

Rorty, Richard (1979) *Philosophy and the Mirror of Nature*. Princeton, NJ, Princeton University Press.

Alvin I. Goldman

Saks, Michael et al. (2001) "Model Prevention and Remedy of Erroneous Convictions Act," *Arizona State Law Journal* **33**, 665–718.

Sokal, Alan and Bricmont, Jean (1998) *Fashionable Nonsense: Postmodern Intellectuals' Abuse of Science*. New York, Picador USA.

Knowledge, Understanding and Epistemic Value

DUNCAN PRITCHARD

1.

It is a widespread pre-theoretical intuition that knowledge is distinctively valuable. If this were not so, then it would be simply *mysterious* why knowledge has been the focus of so much of epistemological theorising, rather than some other epistemic standing like justified true belief. Given this fact, however, it is obviously important to a theory of knowledge that it is able to offer a good explanation of why we have this intuition. Indeed, some, such as Jonathan Kvanvig (2003) and Timothy Williamson (2000), have argued that if a theory of knowledge does not make it transparent why knowledge is distinctively valuable then this is a decisive strike against it. We do not need to go this far, however. What is important is just that a theory of knowledge is able to adequately account for this intuition.

One very direct way of accounting for the intuition would be to offer a theory of knowledge which demonstrated why knowledge is distinctively valuable in the manner that we intuitively suppose. We will call proposals of this sort *validatory*, since they aim to validate our pre-theoretical intuitions about the value of knowledge. Positions of this sort have been offered by, for example, Linda Zagzebski (1996; 1999; 2003) and John Greco (2002; 2007; *forthcominga*), and we will consider one such proposal in this respect below.

Notice, however, that one does not need to validate an intuition in order to account for it. One could instead put forward a theory of knowledge on which knowledge is not distinctively valuable, but which could explain why we might pre-theoretically *think* that knowledge is distinctively valuable. We will call proposals of this sort *revisionist*, since they revise our pre-theoretical intuitions about the value of knowledge. Mark Kaplan (1985), for example, famously argued that the moral of the post-Gettier literature was that it is not knowledge which is distinctively valuable but rather justified true belief − knowledge being justified true belief plus an anti-Gettier condition − but that since justified true belief usually sufficed for knowledge, the mistake was entirely natural. A second proposal

doi:10.1017/S1358246109000046

along these lines, which we will look at in more detail below, is offered by Kvanvig (2003) who argues that it is understanding, not knowledge, which is distinctively valuable, where understanding is an epistemic standing that is closely related to knowledge.

Of course, a final option in this regard is to simply argue that our intuitions on this score are simply wrong on closer analysis. That is, that there is no distinctively valuable epistemic standing. We will call proposals of this sort *fatalist*, since they do not hold out any hope of doing justice to our pre-theoretic intuitions about the value of knowledge in the way that revisionist proposals do. If you think, like Crispin Sartwell (1992), that knowledge just is true belief then you will probably be sympathetic to a view of this sort.[1]

Clearly, a fatalist proposal will be by its nature an uncomfortable position to defend. In this paper I will be exploring a version of validationism and a version of revisionism, and along the way trying to avoid fatalism. As we will see, although both of the proposals that we will be looking at are problematic, a third position will emerge from our discussion which can at least offer us a plausible revisionist account.[2]

2.

The first response that we will be looking at is a form of validationism and it arises out of a certain virtue-theoretic account of knowledge. *Modest* virtue epistemological theories – of the sort defended by, for example, Greco (1999; 2000) in his early work – demand that a necessary condition of knowledge is that the agent forms her true belief via the stable and reliable cognitive abilities that make up her cognitive character. There is obviously a lot to be said about how a proposal of this sort is to be construed. One might build quite a lot into the notion of a cognitive ability, for example, or into the notion of a cognitive character. Depending on how one developed these notions the view could thus be more or less restrictive as an account of knowledge. We can set these issues to one side, however, since, as we will see, what is important for our purposes is the *structure* of a proposal of this sort. The rationale for adding this requirement to a theory of knowledge is that what we primarily want from

[1]   S. Stich 1990 is also often credited with advancing a form of fatalism of this sort about the value of knowledge.
[2]   For more on the problem of accounting for epistemic value, see Pritchard (2007*b*; cf. Pritchard 2007*d*).

such a theory is an account of how we are being suitably sensitive to the facts when we know, and this makes cognitive abilities central to knowledge.

To see this point, consider the following example. Imagine that someone is in a room and forming her beliefs about the temperature of the room by looking at a thermometer on the wall. Suppose further that this is indeed a highly reliable way of forming beliefs in this regard, in the sense that every time she forms her belief in this way the belief so formed is true. Here's the twist. The thermometer is, unbeknownst to the agent, broken, and is fluctuating within a given range. This does not undermine the reliability of the agent's beliefs, however, for the simple reason that there is someone hidden in the room who is altering the thermostat in such a way as to ensure that every time the agent forms a belief about the temperature of the room by looking at the thermostat, her belief is true.

The agent in this case clearly does not have knowledge. Moreover, the right diagnosis of why the agent doesn't know is that the reliability of her belief-forming processes does not reflect any cognitive ability on her part. It is not as if she is being sensitive to the facts in the way that she is forming her beliefs, but rather that the facts are being sensitive to her beliefs – i.e. the direction of fit is all wrong. Virtue epistemology offers a straightforward way of dealing with cases like this, since the fact that the agent is not forming her true belief via her cognitive abilities suffices to entail, on this view, that she lacks knowledge.

Crucially, though, standard forms of virtue epistemology do not regard this appeal to cognitive ability as sufficing to offer a complete account of knowledge. This is because of Gettier-style cases, cases in which something intervenes 'betwixt belief and fact'.[3] Suppose that our agent is looking into a field and, using her reliable cognitive abilities, forms the belief that there is a sheep in the field. Suppose further that this belief is true, but that the agent is not in fact looking at a sheep but a big hairy dog which looks just like a sheep, and which is obscuring from view the sheep that is in the field. The agent in this case clearly lacks knowledge since it is just a matter of luck that her belief is true.[4] Nevertheless, she is forming a true belief via the stable and reliable cognitive abilities that make up her cognitive character.

The standard way in which virtue epistemologists deal with Gettier-style cases is by supplementing the view with an anti-luck

---

[3]   I owe this way of putting the kind of luck in play in Gettier-style cases to P. Unger (1968).

[4]   This example is due to R. Chisholm 1977: 105.

Duncan Pritchard

condition, like the safety principle. This is the move made until quite recently by Greco (1999; 2000), for example (though, as we will see in a moment, Greco takes a very different line on this issue now).[5] We do not need to get into the details of what is involved in a principle like safety here; what is important is just that such a condition ensures that the agent could not have easily been wrong, thereby denying knowledge to agents in the Gettier-style cases.

3.

More recent virtue-epistemic proposals have not taken this line, however, and have instead followed Ernest Sosa (1988; 1991; 2007) in arguing that if we 'beef-up' the ability condition on knowledge then we can deal with Gettier-style cases without appeal to an anti-luck condition. Significantly for our purposes, such a robust virtue epistemology is also able, or so the argument goes at any rate, to account for the distinctive value of knowledge.

Proponents of a robust virtue epistemology of this sort – such as Zagzebski (e.g. 1995) and, in more recent work, Greco (2002; 2007; *forthcominga*; *forthcomingb*) – argue that where modest virtue epistemology goes wrong is by simply requiring the conjunction of cognitive ability and cognitive success (i.e. true belief). So construed, it is possible for something to come 'betwixt' the cognitive ability and the cognitive success such that the success is 'gettierized'. However, we can avoid this situation, they argue, so long as we require not just the conjunction of cognitive success and cognitive ability, but in addition demand that the cognitive success be *because of* cognitive ability, in the sense that the cognitive ability best explains the cognitive success.

Consider again the 'sheep' Gettier-style case described above and suppose that we add the 'because of' requirement. This certainly does seem to deal with this example since while the agent's cognitive success arises out of her cognitive ability, the cognitive success is not *because of* her cognitive ability but rather because of some incidental fact about the environment (i.e. that there happened to be a sheep hidden from view behind the big hairy dog).

So it does seem as if this proposal can indeed deal with Gettier-style cases, and if it can then there is no need to add an anti-luck condition. Of course, adding this requirement will create

---

[5]   For more on safety, see Sosa 1999 and Pritchard 2002; 2005: ch. 6; 2006; 2007a.

problems in other respects, largely due to the fact that it is a complex matter offering the right account of the 'because of' relation. Indeed, on the standard view, the right semantics for causal explanation sentences is along contextualist lines, and this would seem to suggest that a robust virtue epistemology should be allied to a form of attributer contextualism. Although Greco (e.g. *forthcomingb*), for one, has embraced this consequence of his view, this is certainly a surprising alliance. Still, we needn't get bogged-down in this issue.[6] Let us take it that we have at least an intuitive sense of how to read these 'because of' claims. As we will see, the issues that we need to consider in this regard trade on examples where our intuitions are pretty clear-cut, and thus we ought to be able to ignore these complications without too much concern.

4.

The manner in which a proposal of this sort can enable us to deal with the value problem is because knowledge on this view can plausibly be regarded as a type of achievement, and achievements in turn are often thought to be distinctively valuable. Let us consider the notion of an achievement first. Proponents of robust virtue epistemology maintain that an achievement is a success that is because of ability. Since knowledge on their view is to be understood as a cognitive success that is because of cognitive ability, that makes knowledge a cognitive achievement.

In order to see that this is a plausible account of achievement, imagine someone with a bow and arrow selecting a target, firing at that target, and hitting the target. Suppose, however, that the agent in question did not have any ability in this regard. Clearly, in such a case we would not credit the agent with an *achievement*, since it was just dumb luck that she was successful. *A fortiori*, if there is no ability involved then it cannot be because of such ability that the agent is successful and so the account of achievement on offer deals with such cases. Now suppose that we have an agent selecting a target and *skilfully* hitting that target with her arrow. Imagine, however, that the agent's success is gettierized, in that something intervenes 'betwixt' ability and success. Perhaps, for example, a freak gust of wind blows the arrow off course, and then a second gust of wind blows it back on course again. By anyone's lights,

---

[6]   I discuss Greco's view in this regard in more detail in Pritchard (*forthcomingb*).

although the relevant ability is present, we would not say that this success is because of the agent's ability since it is clearly due to the fortuitous second gust of wind. Moreover, by the same token, we would not regard this as an achievement on the part of the agent either, since the success is not properly creditable to her. Again, the account of achievement under consideration deals with such cases. Finally, suppose that the agent's success with the arrow arises out of the relevant skill and is not gettierized. Surely we would now say that this success is because of the archer's ability and, crucially, we would also treat such a success as an achievement, just as the account of achievement on offer would predict.

So there is a good case to be made for thinking that achievements are successes that are because of ability, and if this claim is allowed then the thesis that knowledge is a type of achievement – a cognitive achievement – follows immediately on the robust virtue epistemic view. With this in mind, let us now examine the further claim that achievements are distinctively – indeed, *finally* (i.e. non-instrumentally) – valuable. To begin with, notice that from a practical point of view it might not matter whether or not a success is because of ability, and so constitutes an achievement. If hitting that target wins you the competition, for example, then it may not matter to you whether the success in question was, say, gettierized. Nevertheless, we do value achievements very differently from successes that fall short of being achievements, as when they are gettierized or are due to dumb luck rather than ability. In particular, a genuine achievement seems to be valuable in its own right, independently of any practical value the success in question might generate. For example, all other things being equal, we would surely think that it is better to hit the target because of one's skill than not, even if there is no instrumental value from exhibiting an achievement in this case. This seems to suggest that achievements are *finally* valuable.

If this is right, and knowledge is a type of achievement, then it seems that it will inherit the value of achievements. The reason why knowledge is distinctively valuable is because knowledge is an achievement and achievements are distinctively valuable. This would be a very neat response to the value problem. Moreover, notice that this would be a case in which one's theory of knowledge makes it explicit just why we care about knowledge in the way that we do. As a validationist response to the problem of epistemic value, it is thus very attractive.[7]

---

[7] Interestingly, proponents of this thesis always express the view as being that knowledge is *intrinsically* valuable. Given that the

5.

Now there clearly are some *prima facie* objections to the idea that achievements are finally valuable. Some achievements, after all – such as easy, trivial or wicked achievements – do not seem to be very valuable at all. Notice, however, that the claim is only that achievements are finally valuable *qua* achievements; the thesis is not that all achievements are of *overall* – i.e. all things considered – value. It is thus entirely open to the defender of this thesis to maintain that the overall value of lots of achievements is very low – perhaps negative, if you believe that such a thing is possible – even while defending the specific thesis that achievements are finally valuable.

Alternatively, the proponent of such a thesis could argue for a modified version of the thesis along more holistic lines by saying, for example, that it is in the *nature* of achievements to be finally valuable, even though some achievements, because of their other properties, are not finally valuable.[8] For our purposes, so long as cognitive achievements are the kind of thing that is finally valuable, then that would probably suffice to ensure the distinctive value of knowledge. The thesis that knowledge is distinctively valuable surely does not requires us to claim that *all* knowledge is distinctively valuable. So long as it is in the nature of knowledge, *qua* cognitive achievement, to be finally valuable, then that would almost certainly suffice.

In any case, we can set these issues to one side just now, since there are surely good *prima facie* grounds for thinking that the claim that achievements are distinctively valuable can be adequately motivated. Moreover, the objection I want to raise to this validationist account of epistemic value does not turn on any qualms about the value of achievements but rather concerns the thesis that knowledge should be understood as a cognitive achievement. As we will see, there are good reasons for thinking that such a thesis is unsustainable.

---

non-instrumental value of the cognitive success is due to the relational properties of that success – i.e. due to how that success was achieved – it should be clear that it is specifically final value that is in play here. For more on the distinction between intrinsic and final value, see Rabinowicz & Roennow-Rasmussen 1999; 2003. For more on the distinction as it applies to the debate regarding epistemic value, see Pritchard 2007*d*, ß2.

8   Thanks to Mike Ridge for this suggestion.

6.

Think again about the case of the archer described above. As before, suppose that this archer selects a target at random and skilfully fires at that target, hitting the target as a result of her skill – that is, nothing intervenes 'betwixt' ability and success such that the success is get-tierized. We noted above that in such a case we would surely regard the agent's success as being because of her ability, and therefore credit her with a genuine achievement.

Suppose that we add a further twist to this case, however, and sti-pulate that had the agent chosen any other target on that range then she would have missed because, unbeknownst to her, the targets in question have a forcefield in them which would have deflected the arrows. Her success is thus lucky in the sense that she could have very easily been unsuccessful. Nevertheless, does luck of this sort undermine the agent's achievement? I say not. Indeed, achievements seem entirely compatible with luck of this sort, unlike the Gettier-style luck which intervenes between ability and success. After all, the agent really is hitting the target because of her ability, and the luck in question – which we might term 'environmental' luck – does nothing to undermine this.

Insofar as we grant this point, however, then it creates problems for the knowledge-as-achievement thesis. After all, we can construct an example which is structurally analogous to the one just given but where the environmental luck in question does undermine the agent's putative knowledge. The famous 'barn facade' example is the best illustration of this point. Here we have an agent who sees a barn in clear daylight and so forth and, using her reliable cognitive abilities, forms a belief that what she sees is a barn. Moreover, this belief is true and is not gettierized since she really is looking at a barn (and thus nothing intervenes 'betwixt' belief and fact). Nevertheless, her true belief is epistemically lucky – in the sense that she could have easily been wrong – because unbeknownst to her she is in barn facade county where nearly all the barn-shaped objects are in fact fake barns which are indistinguishable to the naked eye from the real thing. Does our agent know that what she sees is a barn? Surely not, since her true belief is epistemically lucky – she could very easily have been wrong. But is her true belief, her cognitive success, a cognitive achievement? Well, if the 'archer' case just described is anything to go by, then it surely is. After all, her true belief really is because of her cognitive ability, so if that is what constitutes an achievement – and we have seen that there is good reason to think that this is the right way to think about achievements – then we should regard the agent's cognitive success in this case as a cognitive achievement.

It thus seems that sometimes at least there is more to knowledge than a mere cognitive achievement, and this means that the knowledge-as-achievement thesis is false. In particular, it seems that exhibiting a cognitive achievement does not suffice to eliminate all the knowledge-undermining kinds of epistemic luck, such as an environmental epistemic luck.[9]

As far as I am aware, Greco is the only one to have engaged with an objection of this sort – in print, at any rate – and at different points he has made different responses to this objection to his view.[10] Initially, his line was to deny that the agent in the 'barn facade' case – and thus, presumably, the agent in the 'archer' case also – had the ability in question.[11] Abilities are, after all, relative to environments, so this line of argument is not entirely outlandish. Nevertheless, we surely do not want the relativisation of abilities to environments to have the result that abilities must be infallible, and this seems to be the consequence of taking this line (for if the ability is not infallible then there is bound to be a case that we can construct in which the environment is such that the agent could very easily have been wrong). Moreover, neither do we want abilities to be construed in an unduly fine-grained manner such that the relevant ability is lost as soon as one enters the 'deceptive' environment in question.

A second line that Greco (*forthcomingb*) pushed was simply to insist that to say that a success was because of ability is *thereby* to say that it is not due to luck. This is not a helpful suggestion, however, since, as we have seen, while it is plausible to think that the 'because of' eliminates the kind of Gettier-style luck that intervenes 'betwixt' success and ability, it is actually far from obvious – and, indeed, counterintuitive – that it eliminates the very different sort of environmental luck at issue in the cases just given. It seems, then, that one cannot evade a problem like this through stipulation.

Ultimately, however, the line that Greco (2007*b*) has taken to this problem has been to offer further theses regarding the function of our concept of knowledge in order to explain why knowledge, *qua* cognitive achievement, should be more resistant to luck than other

---

[9] For more on this point as it applies to Sosa's view in particular, see Pritchard 2007*c*.

[10] Note that I am not suggesting here that these responses are necessarily in tension with one another; indeed, there is every reason to think that they are complementary.

[11] See Greco *forthcominga*: ß5.

Duncan Pritchard

types of achievement. This move will deal with the problem, but it does beg the question of whether a better way to deal with these cases would be to abandon the knowledge-as-achievement thesis rather than make exceptions for the case of knowledge that do not apply elsewhere.[12]

7.

This problem is even more pressing once one notices that there are cases of knowledge which, intuitively, do not involve cognitive achievements, so that the separation between knowledge and cognitive achievement goes in both directions. Consider the following case, originally offered by Jennifer Lackey (2007), albeit to illustrate a slightly different point.

Imagine our agent getting off the train in an unfamiliar town and asking the first person that she sees for directions. Suppose further that the informant does indeed have first-hand knowledge in this regard and communicates this information to our agent who subsequently heads off to her destination. We would naturally describe such a case as one in which the informant's knowledge was straightforwardly communicated to our agent; indeed, if we don't allow knowledge in cases like this then it seems that quite a lot of our putative testimony-based knowledge is called into question.

Crucially, however, it does not seem at all right to say that our agent's cognitive success is because of *her* cognitive ability. Indeed, the right thing to say seems to be that it is because of the *informant's* cognitive ability, or at least because of their combined cognitive efforts. But that means that sometimes knowledge requires a lot less than a cognitive achievement, contrary to the knowledge-as-achievement thesis.

It is important to be clear what the target of this objection is. Lackey (2007) herself takes it to show that one can have knowledge without it being of *any* credit to one that one has a true belief. But examples like this surely do not license this rather radical conclusion. After all, the agent in this case is exhibiting quite a lot of cognitive ability if one examines the case a little more closely. Although she asks the first person she meets, she wouldn't have asked just *anyone* (or any*thing*). She wouldn't have asked a child, for example, or someone who was clearly a tourist (and she certainly wouldn't have asked a lamppost or a passing dog). Moreover, she is presumably

[12] I discuss Greco's treatment of these issues further in Pritchard *forthcomingb*. See also Kvanvig *forthcoming*.

28

sensitive to potential defeaters. If the informant had given her directions which were obviously fake, for example, then we would have expected her to have spotted this. Indeed, it is only if the agent is exercising her cognitive abilities in this way that it seems permissible to credit her with knowledge.

Nevertheless, the point remains that it is not because of her cognitive abilities that she is cognitively successful – by anyone's lights – even though it is of some credit to her that she is cognitively successful. But this is the point that we need to undermine, the knowledge-as-achievement thesis, since it demonstrates that there is sometimes less to knowledge than a cognitive achievement.

8.

If this were the only problem facing the knowledge-as-achievement thesis, then one might reasonably take the heroic route of denying the intuition in this case and insisting that it is because of the agent's cognitive abilities that she is cognitively successful. But once one combines this objection with that noted earlier – which demonstrates that there is sometimes *more* to knowledge than a cognitive achievement – then this points towards a different way of understanding knowledge.

Indeed, I would argue that what cases like this show is that the modest virtue epistemic proposal is preferable to the robust virtue epistemic proposal. After all, on this view the ability condition on knowledge is not 'beefed up' to the extent that knowledge demands a cognitive achievement, and so one does not get the problem posed by Lackey-style cases. Moreover, since there is also the anti-luck condition on knowledge, expressed in terms of a safety principle, then cases like the barn facade case, in which there is a cognitive achievement but also knowledge-undermining epistemic luck, are also dealt with.

Furthermore, notice that such a view is not necessarily in conflict with the story told by robust virtue epistemologists regarding the distinctive value of knowledge. At the very least, the modest virtue epistemic proposal is consistent with a revisionist response to the problem of epistemic value which says that it is not knowledge, strictly speaking, which is distinctively valuable, but rather cognitive achievement, an epistemic standing which (it seems) only comes apart from knowledge in peripheral cases.

But the modest virtue epistemic proposal might also be compatible with a validationist response to the problem of epistemic value as well.

If it is indeed true that knowledge and cognitive achievement only come apart in peripheral cases – and whether one finds this claim plausible may depend, in part, on one's wider epistemological theory – then one could argue that it is of the nature of knowledge to be distinctively valuable, even though it isn't always distinctively valuable. Perhaps, for example, all paradigm cases of knowledge are also cases of cognitive achievement.[13] If that's right, then there might be scope to argue that knowledge is distinctively valuable after all.

9.

Let us put this tentative conclusion to one side for now, however, because I want to consider a second account of epistemic value which, as we will see, is relevant in this regard. This is the proposal that *understanding* is a distinctively valuable epistemic standing, a thesis which is often supplemented with the further claim that it is the *only* distinctively valuable epistemic standing, thereby making the view a form of revisionism.

It is easy to see the attraction of such a view, in that understanding does seem to be particularly valuable to us. More specifically, insofar as knowledge and understanding do indeed come apart, then understanding seems to be preferable to knowledge. As we might be tempted to put the point, we would surely rather understand than merely know.

Before we can evaluate a claim of this sort, however, we need to be a little clearer about what we are talking about. One problem that afflicts any direct comparison between knowledge and understanding is that knowledge (of the propositional sort that we are concerned with at any rate) is concerned with *propositions*, whereas understanding usually isn't, at least not directly. Interestingly, where understanding is of a proposition, it does seem to be pretty much synonymous with knows. On discovering that my train has been cancelled, I may well say to the person at the ticket office that I understand that the train is cancelled in such a way that I could just as well have used 'know' without any loss. If anything, using 'understand' in this way seems to weaken the effect of the assertion. If I say to you that I understand that you are angry with me then this has the positive effect of being a little less confrontational than a straight assertion that I know that you are angry with me (for one thing, it gives you the option to deny this without obviously accusing me of any ignorance).

---

[13]   I am grateful to Chris Hookway for this suggestion.

Most uses of 'understands' are not like this, however. I want to take the paradigm usage of 'understands' to be in a statement like 'I understand why such-and-such is the case'. Notice that this usage is very different from a more holistic usage which applies to subject matters, as in 'I understand quantum physics', or even 'I understand my wife'. I think the holistic usage of 'understands' is related to the non-holistic, or atomistic, usage that is our focus, but the former raises problems of its own that we've not the space to cover here (though we will flag some of these problems as we go along).[14]

Regarding understanding-why – henceforth just 'understanding' – there are, interestingly, two standard views – a standard view within epistemology and a standard view *outside* of epistemology (particularly in the philosophy of science). The standard view within epistemology is that understanding is distinctively valuable but that it is *not* a species of knowledge. One finds a view of this sort in the work of such figures as Kvanvig (2003), Zagzebski (2001), Wayne Riggs (*forthcoming*) and Catherine Elgin (1996; 2004; *forthcoming*), and we will examine the motivation for such a thesis in a moment.

In contrast, outside of epistemology the consensus is clearly that understanding *is* a species of knowledge. In particular, most philosophers of science who have expressed an opinion on this matter have endorsed the claim that understanding why such-and-such is the case is equivalent to knowing why such-and-such is the case, where this is in turn equivalent to knowing that such-and-such is the case because of such-and-such. So, for example, my understanding of why my house burned down is equivalent to my knowing why my house burned down, where this in turn is tantamount to my knowing that my house burned down because (say) of faulty wiring. One finds a view of this sort – expressed in varying levels of explicitness – in the work of such figures as Peter Achinstein (1983), Wesley Salmon (1989), Philip Kitcher (2002), James Woodward (2003) and Peter Lipton (2004).[15]

---

[14]   For more on holistic and non-holistic conceptions of understanding, see B. Brogaard 2007.

[15]   Consider the following remark made by Lipton 2004: 30 and quoted in S. Grimm 2006: 1, for example: "Understanding is not some sort of super-knowledge, but simply more knowledge: knowledge of causes". The natural way to read this passage is as suggesting that understanding why one's house burned down is just knowing why it burned down – i.e. knowing that it burned down because of (say) faulty wiring. I am grateful to Grimm (2006) for alerting me to some of these references.

As we will see, I want to claim that both of these conceptions of understanding are wrong, at least strictly speaking, and that once we get clear on the relationship between understanding and knowledge we can make some progress towards dealing with the problem of epistemic value.

10.

Let us look first at some the accounts of understanding offered by epistemologists. One guiding theme in this discussion is that understanding is construed along epistemically internalist lines. One extreme example of this can be found in the work of Zagzebski (2001). She argues, amongst other things, that understanding is, unlike knowledge, "transparent" in the sense that there is no gap between seeming to understand and understanding. Relatedly, she also claims that understanding is, unlike knowledge, non-factive, in that even if one's relevant beliefs were false, one's understanding could be unaffected.[16] Finally, she holds that understanding, unlike knowledge, is immune to epistemic luck, in that if one's understanding is subject to such luck it will not thereby be undermined.

Of these claims, the first is clearly the most radical and also, I venture, the one that is most obviously false. To construe understanding in this way seems to reduce it to nothing more than some sort of minimal consistency in one's beliefs, something which might well be transparent to one (though I'm actually doubtful of this). Understanding clearly involves much more than this, however. To see this, let us focus on the non-factivity claim that Zagzebski makes. This claim is also, I will argue, false, but if understanding does imply factivity in the relevant sense, then it will be easy to show that understanding is not transparent in the way that Zagzebski suggests.

To illustrate this point, consider my understanding of why my house has burned down. Let us grant the plausible assumption that this understanding involves a coherent set of relevant beliefs concerning, for example, the faulty wiring in my house. But now suppose that these beliefs are mistaken and that, in particular, there was no faulty

[16]   Riggs (*forthcoming*) and Elgin (*forthcoming*; cf. Elgin 1996; 2004) also argue that understanding is not factive, although their claim is ultimately much weaker than Zagzebski's since it in effect only applies to certain conceptions of understanding (and not, in particular, to the non-holistic conception of understanding in play here).

wiring in my house and so it played no part in the fire. Would we still say that I understand why my house burned down? I think not. For sure, I *thought* I understood – indeed, it could well be that I *reasonably* thought that I understood – but the fact remains that I did not understand. Once one grants that understanding is factive in this way, however, then the transparency claim starts to look equally suspect, since if understanding is factive then it clearly cannot be transparent as the factivity of understanding would require there to be a distinction between thinking that certain facts obtain and their obtaining, contrary to what the transparency thesis demands.

So the transparency and non-factivity claims that Zagzebski offers are false. It is difficult to diagnose why Zagzebski made this mistake. Part of the reason may be that there is a failure to be clear about the type of understanding under consideration. After all, when it comes to the kind of holistic understanding that applies to a subject matter, this plausibly *is* compatible with at least *some* false beliefs about that subject matter, but this sort of understanding is precisely not the sort at issue. Moreover, it would seem that the analogue of Zagzebski's non-factivity claim as regards understanding when it comes to holistic understanding would be that such understanding can be possessed even though one has *no* relevant true beliefs, and that is surely implausible.[17]

More generally, however, I think the diagnosis for where Zagzebski's conception of understanding goes awry lies in overstating the internalist aspect of understanding. Understanding clearly is very amenable to an account along internalist lines, in the sense that it is hard to make sense of how an agent could possess understanding and yet lack good reflectively accessible grounds in support of that understanding. Understanding thus cannot be 'opaque' to the subject in the way that knowledge, by externalist lights at least, can sometimes be. Granting this, however, does not entail that one should regard understanding as non-factive, much less transparent.

[17] It should be noted that there are some good arguments offered by Elgin (*forthcoming*) in this respect regarding the growth of understanding within false scientific theories, and the use of idealisations in scientific thinking, which might seem to suggest a conception of holistic understanding which is entirely non-factive. It would take us too far afield to consider these arguments, however, and Zagzebski clearly doesn't have considerations like this in mind when she offers her conception of (non-holistic) understanding. For my own part, I think that even here we should say that genuine understanding entails a system of beliefs which is broadly correct, at least as regards the beliefs that are fundamental to that system. For more on this point, see Pritchard 2007b: ß5.

Duncan Pritchard

11.

With this in mind, let us consider a second account of understanding in the epistemological literature – due to Kvanvig (2003) – which does not succumb to the mistakes made by Zagzebski's account. Zagzebski holds that both knowledge and understanding are distinctively valuable. In contrast, Kvanvig maintains that it is only understanding that is distinctively valuable, where understanding is distinct from knowing.

Unlike Zagzebski, Kvanvig does not hold that understanding is transparent or non-factive. He does, however, treat the notion along internalist lines which, as we've just noted, is entirely proper. The way in which he distinguishes knowledge from understanding is primarily through two further claims. The first is that understanding, unlike knowledge, admits of degrees. The second is that understanding, unlike knowledge, is immune to epistemic luck, a thesis which we saw Zagzebski putting forward a moment ago.

The import of the first claim is, I think, moot. After all, even if this is true, it needn't follow that there are cases of knowledge which aren't corresponding cases of understanding, or that there are cases of understanding which aren't corresponding cases of knowledge. The weight of the distinction between knowledge and understanding on this view thus falls on the second claim, which merits further consideration.

This thesis is meant to reflect, I think, the internalist dimension to understanding. That is, the idea is that just as one's justification, internalistically conceived, is not undermined by epistemic luck (just the sufficiency of that justification, with true belief, for knowledge), so one's understanding is not undermined either. Closer inspection of this claim reveals that the relationship between understanding and epistemic luck is, however, more complex than Kvanvig and Zagzebski suppose.

The example that Kvanvig offers to illustrate this claim is that of someone who, by reading a book on the Comanche tribe, gains a series of beliefs about the Comanche and, thereby, an "historical understanding of the Comanche dominance of the southern plains of North America from the late seventeenth until the late nineteenth century" (Kvanvig 2003: 197).[18] We are told that the relevant class of beliefs contains no falsehood, and that the agent can answer all the

---

[18]   Understanding of this very general claim might start to look dangerously close to holistic understanding of a subject matter, rather than the non-holistic understanding that we are interested in here. In what follows, I will set this concern to one side and simply read it as non-holistic understanding.

relevant questions correctly in this regard (thereby illustrating that the putative knowledge possessed is not 'opaque'). However, Kvanvig argues that although in such a case one would expect the agent to have knowledge of the relevant beliefs, this is not essential − it could well be, as he points out, that the true beliefs in question have been 'gettierized', perhaps because the information that the agent has is only "accidentally true" (*ibid.*).

I think that a case like this is crucially ambiguous, but we can get a better handle on what is going on here by taking a simpler case and then returning to consider this more complex example in the light of our intuitions as regards the simpler case.

Consider the example of understanding why one's house burned down. Suppose first that we have a standard Gettier-style case in which something intervenes 'betwixt' belief and fact. For example, imagine that, upon finding one's house in flames, one approaches someone who looks as if she is the fire officer in charge and asks her what the reason for the fire is. Suppose one is told by this person that the reason why one's house is burning is faulty wiring, and this coheres with one's wider set of beliefs. But suppose now that the person one asked in this regard is not in fact the fire officer in charge but instead someone who is simply dressed in a fire officer's uniform and who is on her way to a fancy dress party. Still, one did indeed gain a true belief in this regard. So, even though the epistemic luck in question prevents one from having knowledge of the relevant propositions, does one lose one's understanding? Seemingly, it does, for ask yourself the question now of whether you understand why your house burnt down. Surely the answer to this question is a straightforward 'no'. One cannot gain an understanding of why one's house burnt down by consulting someone who, unbeknownst to you, is not the fire officer but instead someone in fancy dress.

12.

So does this mean that Kvanvig is just wrong in thinking that understanding is immune to epistemic luck? Not entirely since, as we have noted above, there is a kind of epistemic luck which is knowledge-undermining but which is not of the sort that appears in Gettier-style cases which intervenes 'betwixt' belief and fact. With this in mind, consider a variant on the case just described in which it is not Gettier-style epistemic luck that is at issue but rather the sort of 'environmental' epistemic luck at issue in the barn facade case. For example, imagine that the apparent fire officer that one asks about the cause of the fire is indeed the fire officer, but that one could nevertheless have been easily wrong because there were other people in the vicinity dressed as fire officers – all going to the same fancy dress party, say – who one could very easily have asked and who would have given one a false answer (while failing to indicate that they were not real fire officers).

In such a case, as we saw above, one's cognitive success would be because of one's cognitive abilities, and so would constitute a cognitive achievement, and yet the epistemic luck at issue would prevent it from counting as knowledge. The critical question for us, however, is whether it is a case of understanding. I want to argue that it is, and thus that Kvanvig is right on at least this score: 'environmental' epistemic luck, unlike Gettier-style epistemic luck, *is* compatible with possessing understanding. After all, the agent concerned has all the true beliefs required for understanding why his house burned down, and also acquired this understanding in the right fashion. It is thus hard to see why the mere presence of 'environmental' epistemic luck should deprive the agent of understanding.

With this distinction between two types of epistemic luck in mind – one, the Gettier-style epistemic luck, which is inconsistent with understanding and a second, the 'environmental' epistemic luck, which is consistent with understanding – we can return to evaluate Kvanvig's 'Comanche' case. Whether or not the agent retains her understanding in this case will depend on the type of epistemic luck at issue.

So, for example, suppose that the agent forms her beliefs about the Comanches by reading an apparently scholarly book which is in fact nothing of the sort. Let us say, for instance, that the author of this book simply took lots of rumours and unchecked stories about the Comanche and presented them, along with some inventive guesswork, as established fact. But suppose further that despite this lack of attention to scholarship, the author did get matters entirely right. This would thus be a Gettier-style case in which our agent gains lots of true beliefs about the Comanches: she has good reason to think that her beliefs about the Comanche are true, and they are true, but it is just a matter of luck that they are true given that the source of these beliefs is so unreliable. Can one gain an understanding of the Comanche tribe in this way? In particular, can one gain an historical understanding of why the Comanche were so dominant in the southern plains of North America from the late seventeenth until the late nineteenth century in this fashion? I want to suggest that one cannot, any more than one can gain an understanding of why one's house burnt down by gaining a true belief about what caused the fire from someone pretending to be a fire officer.

Matters are different, however, if we redescribe the case as a form of environmental epistemic luck, rather than as Gettier-style epistemic luck. Suppose, for example, that the book that the agent consults is indeed appropriately scholarly – and thus reliable – when it comes to this subject-matter, and that the agent accordingly gains lots of true beliefs about the Comanche. Nevertheless, the luck enters the picture because of how all the other books on this topic – which are also superficially just as a scholarly – are very unreliable, and one could very easily have found out what one did by consulting one of these books. Does epistemic luck of this sort undermine one's understanding in the way that it would undermine one's knowledge? I don't think that it does, since one did indeed find out the relevant facts in the right kind of way. Just as one can gain an understanding of why one's house burnt down by speaking to the fire officer – even though one could just have easily been misled by someone who isn't the fire officer – so one can gain an understanding of the Comanche by reading a reliable book even though one could have very easily consulted an unreliable book.[19]

13.

So while Kvanvig and others are right to think that understanding is compatible with a certain type of knowledge-undermining epistemic luck, they are wrong to think that it is compatible with all types of knowledge-undermining epistemic luck. Their mistake, it seems, is to fail to distinguish between two crucial ways in which epistemic luck can be knowledge-undermining. That understanding is compatible with one type of knowledge-undermining epistemic luck suffices, however, to show that knowledge is distinct from understanding, since it entails that one can have understanding without the associated knowledge.

---

[19]   While noticing that Kvanvig's claim that understanding is compatible with epistemic luck is not quite right, Grimm 2006 fails to recognise that the mistake here is simply to equate environmental epistemic luck with Gettier-style epistemic luck. As a result, he concludes that understanding is just as incompatible with epistemic luck as knowledge is, and thus that knowledge is a species of understanding after all.

Duncan Pritchard

One consequence of this is that the standard view of understanding outside of epistemology, such that understanding is a species of knowledge, is false. Indeed, this is not the only respect in which this conception of understanding is mistaken. Recall that on this conception of understanding, to understand why such-and-such is the case is equivalent to knowing why such-and-such is the case, which is in turn equivalent to knowing that such-and-such is the case because of such-and-such. As we have seen, however, the problem of environmental epistemic luck illustrates that I can understand why my house burned down even while failing to know why it burned down (indeed, even while failing to know that it burned down because of faulty wiring).

There is also a second respect in which this conception of understanding is mistaken, since it is possible to know why one's house has burned down (and indeed know that it burned down because of faulty wiring), even though one does not understand why one's house burned down. We can illustrate this point via a Lackey-style example. Suppose that I understand why my house burned down, know why it burned down, and also know that it burned down because of faulty wiring. Imagine further that my young son asks me why his house burned down and I tell him. He has no conception of how faulty wiring might cause a fire, so we could hardly imagine that merely knowing this much suffices to afford him understanding of why his house burned down. Nevertheless, he surely does know that his house burned down because of faulty wiring, and thus also knows why his house burned down. Indeed, we can imagine a teacher asking my son if he knows why his house burned down and him telling the teacher the reason. If asked by a second teacher if my son knew why his house burned down, we could then imagine the first teacher saying that he did. So, it seems, one can not only have understanding without the corresponding knowledge, but also knowledge without the corresponding understanding.[20]

14.

Just as the Lackey-style case offered earlier demonstrated that sometimes one might have knowledge without a cognitive achievement, the same moral can be drawn here. My son might know why his

[20] For more on the relationship between understanding and knowing-why, see Pritchard *forthcomingc*.

house burned down, but this knowledge does not constitute a cognitive achievement on his part because of how he is unable to take appropriate credit for the truth of his belief. Interestingly, however, we have just seen that while knowledge and cognitive achievement come apart on this score, understanding and cognitive achievement do not. My son's knowledge does not constitute a cognitive achievement, but then neither does it constitute genuine understanding on his part either.[21]

Indeed, we have good reason to think that all understanding involves cognitive achievement. Recall that the moral of the barn facade case described earlier was that one could exhibit a cognitive achievement and yet lack knowledge, because of how knowledge, unlike cognitive achievement, is incompatible with environmental epistemic luck. The same applies to understanding. When one couples this observation with the fact that the cases in which an agent has knowledge while not exhibiting a cognitive achievement are cases in which the agent lacks the relevant understanding, then one can see that there is a strong *prima facie* case for thinking that all understanding involves a cognitive achievement.

Indeed, I think this thesis is highly plausible. Its plausibility relates to the fact that understanding seems to be essentially an epistemically internalist notion, in the sense that if one has understanding then it should not be opaque to one that one has this understanding – in particular, one should have good reflectively accessible grounds in support of the relevant beliefs that undergird that understanding. But given that this is a requirement of understanding, it is unsurprising that one can construct a Lackey-style case in which an agent has knowledge but not understanding, since such cases work precisely by using examples of agents who, while having knowledge, lack good reflectively accessible grounds in favour of their beliefs.

That understanding is both factive and resistant to Gettier-style epistemic luck also demonstrates, however, that we should be wary of construing understanding along purely internalist lines. One's reflectively accessible grounds in favour of one's belief might well survive the falsity of what one believes and also be compatible with Gettier-style luck, but as we have seen, the same is not true of understanding. Just as genuine cognitive achievements do not depend exclusively on the cognitive efforts of the agent, but also on the relevant cognitive success and the right connection obtaining between

---

[21]   I argue in Pritchard *forthcominga* that this point has some important implications for the epistemology of testimony.

cognitive ability and cognitive success, so genuine understanding makes the same 'external' demands.

15.

So where does all this leave us as regards the problem of epistemic value? Recall that we noted above that the robust virtue epistemic approach to this problem did not succeed, in that there was no straightforward way of showing that the distinctive value of cognitive achievements carried over to knowledge. At most, this approach demonstrated that it is cognitive achievements that are distinctively valuable but, since one could exhibit a cognitive achievement while lacking knowledge, and know while failing to exhibit a cognitive achievement, this thesis, unless suitably supplemented with further argument at any rate, did not translate into the claim that knowledge is distinctively valuable. Indeed, as matters stand, what we end up with is a kind of revisionism rather than a form of validationism, in that it is actually cognitive achievements that are distinctively valuable, rather than knowledge.

We have noted here that understanding also comes apart from knowledge, in the sense that one can have understanding while lacking the corresponding knowledge and have knowledge while lacking the corresponding understanding. Nevertheless, if cognitive achievements are the kind of thing which are distinctively valuable, then – given that we have seen that there are strong grounds for supposing that understanding is a kind of cognitive achievement – we have a straightforward explanation of why understanding is distinctively valuable.

At the very least, then, we have a form of revisionism available to us which could explain why understanding, rather than knowledge, is distinctively valuable. Interestingly for our purposes, however, a form of revisionism which appeals to the special value of understanding is, I think, more appealing than a form of revisionism which appeals to an epistemic standing which is clearly a 'lesser' epistemic standing when assessed relative to knowledge, such as justified true belief. For while one can have understanding while lacking knowledge, it should be clear that understanding requires an intellectual sophistication that is not necessarily demanded by knowledge. One can imagine, for example, an agent knowing a great deal while having very little understanding of anything, but it is hard to imagine the converse. If understanding is a cognitive achievement, something that can only fall short of knowledge when environmental epistemic luck is present, then we have a straightforward explanation for this intuition. Knowledge may or may not be distinctively valuable, but understanding certainly is, and given the features of understanding that we have noted, this claim, while in itself revisionist, is certainly highly plausible.[22]

Edinburgh University

References

Achinstein, P. (1983) *The Nature of Explanation*, Oxford University Press, Oxford.

Brogaard, B. (2007) "I Know. Therefore, I Understand", *typescript*.

Chisholm, R. (1977) *Theory of Knowledge* (2nd Ed.), Prentice-Hall, Englewood Cliffs, New Jersey.

Elgin, C. (1996) *Considered Judgement*, Princeton University Press, Princeton, NJ.

————— (2004) "True Enough", *Philosophical Issues* **14**, 113–31.

————— (*Forthcoming*). "Is Understanding Factive?", *Epistemic Value*, (eds.) A. Haddock, A. Millar & D. H. Pritchard, Oxford University Press, Oxford.

Greco, J. (1999) "Agent Reliabilism", *Philosophical Perspectives* **13**, 273–96.

————— (2000) *Putting Skeptics in Their Place: The Nature of Skeptical Arguments and Their Role in Philosophical Inquiry*, Cambridge University Press, Cambridge, UK.

————— (2002) "Knowledge as Credit for True Belief", *Intellectual Virtue: Perspectives from Ethics and Epistemology*, (eds.) M. DePaul & L. Zagzebski, Oxford University Press, Oxford.

————— (2007) "The Nature of Ability and the Purpose of Knowledge", *typescript*.

[22] An earlier version of this paper was presented at the *Royal Institute of Philosophy* as part of the *Epistemology* lecture series in 2006 and at a departmental talk at the University of Edinburgh in 2007. I am grateful to the audiences on these occasions, especially Sharar Ali, Matthew Chrisman, Andy Clark, Jennifer Hornsby, Jesper Kallestrup, Anthony O'Hear, Mike Ridge and Barry Smith. Special thanks go to Ernie Sosa, who commented on an earlier draft. This paper has benefited from an AHRC Research Leave award.

Duncan Pritchard

————— (*Forthcominga*) "The Value Problem", in *The Value of Knowledge*, (eds.) A. Haddock, A. Millar, & D. H. Pritchard, Oxford University Press, Oxford.

————— (*Forthcomingb*) "What's Wrong With Contextualism?", *The Philosophical Quarterly*.

Grimm, S. (2006) "Is Understanding a Species of Knowledge?", *British Journal for the Philosophy of Science* **57**, 515–35.

Kitcher, P. (2002) "Scientific Knowledge", in *Oxford Handbook of Epistemology*, (ed.) P. Moser, Oxford University Press, Oxford.

Kvanvig, J. (2003) *The Value of Knowledge and the Pursuit of Understanding*, Cambridge University Press, Cambridge, UK.

————— (*Forthcoming*) "Responses", in *The Value of Knowledge*, (eds.) A. Haddock, A. Millar, & D. H. Pritchard, Oxford University Press, Oxford.

Lackey, J. (2007) "Why We Don't Deserve Credit for Everything We Know", *Synthese* **156**.

Lipton, P. (2004) *Inference to the Best Explanation*, Routledge, London.

Pritchard, D. H. (2002). "Resurrecting the Moorean Response to the Sceptic", *International Journal of Philosophical Studies* **10**, 283–307.

————— (2005) *Epistemic Luck*, Oxford University Press, Oxford.

————— (2006) "Knowledge, Luck and Lotteries", in *New Waves in Epistemology*, (eds.) V. F. Hendricks & D. H. Pritchard, Palgrave Macmillan, London.

————— (2007*a*) "Anti-Luck Epistemology", *Synthese* **156**.

————— (2007*b*) "Recent Work on Epistemic Value", *American Philosophical Quarterly*, **44**, 85–110.

————— (2007*c*) "Sosa On Epistemic Value", 2nd On-Line Philosophy Conference, http://experimentalphilosophy.typepad.com/2nd_annual_online_philoso/2007/05/ernest_sosa.html

————— (2007*d*) "The Value of Knowledge", *typescript*.

————— (*Forthcominga*). "A Defence of Quasi-Reductionism in the Epistemology of Testimony", *Philosophica*.

————— (*Forthcomingb*) "Greco on Knowledge: Virtues, Contexts, Achievements", *The Philosophical Quarterly*.

————— (*Forthcomingc*) "Knowing the Answer, Understanding and Epistemic Value", *Grazer Philosophische Studien*.

Rabinowicz, W., & Roennow-Rasmussen, T. (1999) "A Distinction in Value: Intrinsic and For its Own Sake", *Proceedings of the Aristotelian Society* **100**, 33–49.

————— (2003) "Tropic of Value", *Philosophy and Phenomenological Research* **66**, 389–403.

Riggs, W. (*Forthcoming*) "Getting the *Meno* Requirement Right", in *Epistemic Value*, (eds.) A. Haddock, A. Millar & D. H. Pritchard, Oxford University Press, Oxford.

Salmon, W. (1989) "Four Decades of Scientific Explanation", *Minnesota Studies in the Philosophy of Science* 13.

Sartwell, C. (1992) "Why Knowledge is Merely True Belief", *Journal of Philosophy*, **89**, 167–80.

Sosa, E. (1988) "Beyond Skepticism, to the Best of our Knowledge", *Mind* 97, 153–89.

————— (1991) *Knowledge in Perspective: Selected Essays in Epistemology*, Cambridge University Press, Cambridge, UK.

————— (1999) "How to Defeat Opposition to Moore", *Philosophical Perspectives* 13, 141–54.

————— (2007) *A Virtue Epistemology: Apt Belief and Reflective Knowledge*, Oxford University Press, Oxford.

Stich, S. (1990) *The Fragmentation of Reason*, MIT Press, Cambridge, MA.

Unger, P. (1968) "An Analysis of Factual Knowledge", *Journal of Philosophy* **65**, 157–70.

Williamson, T. (2000) *Knowledge and its Limits*, Oxford University Press, Oxford.

Woodward, J. (2003) *Making Things Happen: A Theory of Causal Explanation*, Oxford University Press, Oxford.

Zagzebski, L. (1996) *Virtues of the Mind: An Inquiry into the Nature of Virtue and the Ethical Foundations of Knowledge*, Cambridge University Press, Cambridge, UK.

————— (1999) "What is Knowledge?", in *The Blackwell Guide to Epistemology*, (eds.) J. Greco & E. Sosa, 92–116, Blackwell, Oxford.

————— (2001) "Recovering Understanding", in *Knowledge, Truth and Duty: Essays on Epistemic Justification, Responsibility and Virtue*, (ed.) M. Steup, Oxford University Press, Oxford.

————— (2003) "The Search for the Source of the Epistemic Good", *Metaphilosophy* **34**, 12–28; and reprinted in *Moral and Epistemic Virtues*, (eds.) M. S. Brady & D. H. Pritchard, 13–28, Blackwell, Oxford (2003).

Knowledge of Counterfactuals

TIMOTHY WILLIAMSON

Here are two claims:

(0I)   If my enemies tried to murder me yesterday, they failed.

(0)   If my enemies had tried to murder me yesterday, they would have failed.

In some sense that requires clarification, the antecedent of the indicative conditional (0I) supposes that my enemies *actually* tried to murder me, while the antecedent of the 'subjunctive' or 'counterfactual' conditional (0) supposes only that they tried to murder me in hypothetical circumstances without supposing those circumstances to be actual. I can easily know (0I) because I know that I am still alive. It is harder for me to know (0). Perhaps my enemies are clever and determined; my evidence may indicate that if they had tried, they would have succeeded. That I am still alive indicates that they did not try to murder me, not that they would have failed if they had tried. But (0) is not impossible to know. Perhaps, instead, I have bugged my enemies' discussions, and know that the murder plan they have ready for me depends on a false assumption about my whereabouts. Yet knowledge of such counterfactuals is puzzling. We cannot observe things that might have happened but didn't; nor can we observe their causes or effects.

Knowledge of counterfactuals has a special significance for philosophy. For many philosophical claims concern whether something that does not occur nevertheless could have occurred: for instance, time without space. In the jargon, they concern metaphysical possibility, impossibility and necessity. Our knowledge of these matters, such as it is, has grown out of our knowledge of far more mundane counterfactual matters, such as (0).

The aim of this essay is to sketch a picture of our ordinary knowledge of counterfactuals, and then to use it to raise a problem for the traditional philosophical dichotomy between *a priori* and *a posteriori* knowledge.[1]

---

[1]   For the relation of the present account to knowledge of metaphysical modality see Williamson 2007, on which this paper draws.

doi:10.1017/S135824610900006X

Timothy Williamson

We can usefully start with a well-known example which proves the term 'counterfactual conditional' misleading. To adapt an example from Alan Ross Anderson (1951: 37), a doctor might say:

(1)   If Jones had taken arsenic, he would have shown such-and-such symptoms.

We observe:

(2)   Jones shows such-and-such symptoms.

Clearly, (1) and (2) can provide abductive evidence by inference to the best explanation for the antecedent of (1) (see Edgington 2003: 23–7 for more discussion):

(3)   Jones took arsenic.

If further tests subsequently verify (3), they confirm the doctor's statement rather than in any way falsifying it or making it inappropriate. If we still call subjunctive conditionals like (1) 'counterfactuals', the reason is not that they imply or presuppose the falsity of their antecedents. Rather, what the antecedent of (1) does not suppose is that Jones *actually* took arsenic. In what follows, we shall be just as concerned with conditional sentences such as (1) as with those whose premises are false, or believed to be so.

While (1) adds valuable empirical evidence to (2), the corresponding indicative conditional does not:

(1I)   If Jones took arsenic, he shows such-and-such symptoms.

We can safely assent to (1I) just on the basis of inspecting Jones's corpse and observing (2), before hearing what the doctor has to say, simply because we can see that Jones *does* show such-and-such symptoms, whether or not he took arsenic. Informally, (1) is more useful than (1I) because (1), unlike (1I), depends on a comparison between independently specified terms, the symptoms Jones would have shown if he had taken arsenic and the symptoms he does in fact show. Thus the process of evaluating the 'counterfactual' conditional requires something like two files, one for the actual situation, the other for the counterfactual situation, even if these situations turn out to coincide. No such cross-comparison of files is needed to evaluate the indicative conditional, given (2). Of course, when one evaluates an indicative conditional while disbelieving its antecedent, one must not confuse one's file of beliefs with one's file of judgments on the supposition of the antecedent, but that does not mean that cross-referencing from the latter file to the former can play the role it did in the counterfactual case.

Since (1) constitutes empirical evidence, its truth was not guaranteed in advance. If Jones had looked suitably different, the doctor would have had to assert the opposite counterfactual conditional:

(4)   If Jones had taken arsenic, he would not have shown such-and-such symptoms.

From (2) and (4) we can deduce (5), the negation of its antecedent, for a counterfactual conditionals with a true antecedent and a false consequent is false:

(5)   Jones did not take arsenic.

The indicative conditional corresponding to (4) is:

(4I)   If Jones took arsenic, he does not show such-and-such symptoms.

Since we can clearly see that Jones does show such-and-such symptoms, to assert (4I) is like saying 'If Jones took arsenic, pigs can fly'. Although a very confident doctor might assert (4I), on the grounds that Jones certainly did not take arsenic, that certainty may in turn be based on confidence in (4), and therefore on the comparison of actual and counterfactual situations.

We also use the notional distinction between actual and counterfactual situations to make evaluative comparisons:

(6)   If Jones had not taken arsenic, he would have been in better shape than he now is.

Such counterfactual reflections facilitate learning from experience; one may decide never to take arsenic oneself. Formulating counterfactuals about past experience is empirically correlated with improved future performance in various tasks.[2]

Evidently, counterfactual conditionals give clues to causal connections. This point does not commit one to any ambitious programme of analysing causality in terms of counterfactual conditionals (Lewis 1973, Collins, Hall and Paul 2004), or counterfactual conditionals in terms of causality (Jackson 1977). If the former programme succeeds, all causal thinking is counterfactual thinking; if the latter succeeds, all counterfactual thinking is causal thinking. Either way, the overlap is so large that we cannot have one without much of the other. It may well be over-optimistic to expect either necessary and

---

[2]   The large empirical literature on the affective role of counterfactuals and its relation to learning from experience includes Kahneman and Tversky 1982, Roese and Olson 1993, 1995 and Byrne 2005.

Timothy Williamson

sufficient conditions for causal statements in counterfactual terms or necessary and sufficient conditions for counterfactual statements in causal terms. Even so, counterfactuals surely play a crucial role in our causal thinking (see Harris 2000: 118–139 and Byrne 2005: 100–128 for some empirical discussion). Only extreme sceptics deny the cognitive value of causal thought.

At a more theoretical level, claims of nomic necessity support counterfactual conditionals. If it is a law that property P implies property Q, then typically if something were to have P, it would have Q. If we can falsify the counterfactual in a specific case, perhaps by using better-established laws, we thereby falsify that claim of lawhood. We sometimes have enough evidence to establish what the result of an experiment would be without actually doing the experiment: that matters in a world of limited resources.

Counterfactual thought is deeply integrated into our empirical thought in general. Although that consideration will not deter the most dogged sceptics about our knowledge of counterfactuals, it indicates the difficulty of preventing such scepticism from generalizing implausibly far, since our beliefs about counterfactuals are so well-integrated into our general knowledge of our environment. I proceed on the assumption that we have non-trivial knowledge of counterfactuals.

In discussing the epistemology of counterfactuals, I assume no particular theory of the semantics of the counterfactual conditional. In particular, I do not assume the Stalnaker-Lewis approach, on which a counterfactual conditional statement is true in a given possible world if and only if either the consequent is true in the closest possible world or worlds to the given one or (the vacuous case) the antecedent is false in all possible worlds, where closeness is measured by similarity in certain respects (Stalnaker 1968, Lewis 1979, 1986). However, the Stalnaker-Lewis approach will occasionally be used for purposes of illustration and vividness. That evasion of semantic theory might seem dubious, since it is the semantics which determines what has to be known. However, we can go some way on the basis of our pretheoretical understanding of such conditionals in our native language. Moreover, the best developed formal semantic theories of counterfactuals use an apparatus of possible worlds or situations at best distantly related to our actual cognitive processing. While that does not refute such theories, which concern the truth-conditions of counterfactuals, not how subjects attempt to find out whether those truth-conditions obtain, it shows how indirect the relation between the semantics and the epistemology may be. When we come to fine-tune our epistemology of counterfactuals, we may need an articulated semantic theory, but at a first pass we can make do with some sketchy remarks about their epistemology while remaining neutral over their deep semantic analysis. As for the psychological study of the processes underlying our assessment of counterfactual conditionals, it remains in a surprisingly undeveloped state, as recent authors have complained (Evans and Over 2004: 113–131).

Start with an example. You are in the mountains. As the sun melts the ice, rocks embedded in it are loosened and crash down the slope. You notice one rock slide into a bush. You wonder where it would have ended if the bush had not been there. A natural way to answer the question is by visualizing the rock sliding without the bush there, then bouncing down the slope into the lake at the bottom. Under suitable background conditions, you thereby come to know this counterfactual:

(7)   If the bush had not been there, the rock would have ended in the lake.

You could test that judgment by physically removing the bush and experimenting with similar rocks, but you know (7) even without performing such experiments. Logically, the counterfactual about the past is independent of claims about future experiments (for a start, the slope is undergoing continual small changes).

Somehow, you came to know the counterfactual by using your imagination. That sounds puzzling if one conceives the imagination as unconstrained. You can imagine the rock rising vertically into the air, or looping the loop, or sticking like a limpet to the slope. What constrains imagining it one way rather than another?

You do not imagine it those other ways because your imaginative exercise is radically informed and disciplined by your perception of the rock and the slope and your sense of how nature works. The default for the imagination may be to proceed as 'realistically' as it can, subject to whatever deviations the thinker imposes by brute force: here, the absence of the bush. Thus the imagination can in principle exploit all our background knowledge in evaluating counterfactuals. Of course, how to separate background knowledge from what must be imagined away in imagining the antecedent is Goodman's old, deep problem of cotenability (1954). For example, why don't we bring to bear our background knowledge that the rock did not go far, and imagine another obstacle to its fall? Difficult though the problem is, it should not make us lose sight of our considerable knowledge of counterfactuals: our procedures for evaluating them cannot be too wildly misleading.

Timothy Williamson

Can the imaginative exercise be regimented as a piece of reasoning? We can undoubtedly assess some counterfactuals by straightforward reasoning. For instance:

(8)   If twelve people had come to the party, more than eleven people would have come to the party.

We can deduce the consequent 'More than eleven people came to the party' from the antecedent 'Twelve people came to the party', and assert (8) on that basis. Similarly, it may be suggested, we can assert (7) on the basis of inferring its consequent 'The rock ended in the lake' from the premise 'The bush was not there', given auxiliary premises about the rock, the mountainside and the laws of nature.

At the level of formal logic, we have the corresponding plausible and widely accepted closure principle that, given a derivation of a conclusion from some premises, we can derive the counterfactual conditional that if a specified state of affairs had obtained the conclusion would have held from counterfactual conditionals to the effect that if the state of affairs had obtained the premises would have held; in other words, the counterfactual consequences of a supposition are closed under logical consequence. With the trivial principle that if a state of affairs had obtained it would have obtained, it follows that, given a derivation of a conclusion from the supposition that a specified state of affairs obtains alone, we need no extra premises to derive the counterfactual conditional that if the state of affairs had obtained the conclusion would have held.

We cannot automatically extend the closure rule to the case where there are auxiliary premises. For example, from the premises 'She won the match' and 'She broke her leg' we can trivially derive the conclusion 'She won the match', but we cannot legitimately move from that to deriving the counterfactual conclusion 'If she had broken her leg she would have won the match' from the premise 'She won the match', since the latter may be true when the former is false. Auxiliary premises cannot always be copied into the scope of counterfactual suppositions (this is the problem of cotenability again).

Even with this caution, the treatment of the process by which we reach counterfactual judgments as inferential is problematic in several ways. Two will be discussed here.

First, the putative reasoner may lack general-purpose cognitive access to the auxiliary premises of the putative reasoning. In particular, the folk physics needed to derive the consequents of counterfactuals such as (7) from their antecedents may be stored in the form of some analogue mechanism, perhaps embodied in a connectionist network, which the subject cannot articulate in propositional form. Normally, a subject who uses negation and derives a conclusion from some premises can at least entertain the negation of a given premise, whether or not they are willing to assert it, perhaps on the basis of the other premises and the negation of the conclusion. Our reliance on folk physics does not enable us to formulate its negation. More generally, the supposed premises may not be stored in a form that permits the normal range of inferential interactions with other beliefs, even at an unconscious level. This strains the analogy with explicit reasoning.

The other problem is epistemological. Normally, someone who believes a conclusion on the sole basis of inference from some premises knows the conclusion only if they know the premises. This principle must be applied with care, for often a thinker is aware of several inferential routes from different sets of premises to the same conclusion. For example, you believe that a and b are F; you deduce that something is F. If you know that a is F, you may thereby come to know that something is F, even if your belief that b is F is false, and so not knowledge. Similarly, you may believe more premises than you need to draw an inductive conclusion. The principle applies only to essential premises, those that figure in all the inferences on which the relevant belief in the conclusion is based. However, folk physics is an essential standing background premise of the supposed inferences from antecedents to consequents of counterfactuals like (7), as usually conceived, so the epistemological maxim applies. Folk physics in this sense is a theory whose content includes the general principles by which expectations of motion, constancy and the like are formed on-line in real time; it is no mere collection of memories of particular past incidents. But then presumably it is strictly speaking false: although many of its predictions are useful approximations, they are inaccurate in some circumstances; knowledge of the true laws of motion is not already wired into our brains, otherwise physics could be reduced to psychology. Since folk physics is false, it is not known. But the conclusion that no belief formed on the basis of folk physics constitutes knowledge is wildly sceptical. For folk physics is reliable enough in many circumstances to be used in the acquisition of knowledge, for example that the cricket ball will land in that field. Thus we should not conceive folk physics as a premise of that conclusion. Nor should we conceive some local fragment of folk physics as the premise. For it would be quite unmotivated to take an inferential approach overall while refusing to treat this local fragment as itself derived from the general theory of folk physics. We should conceive folk physics as a locally but not globally reliable method of belief formation, not as a premise.

If folk theories are methods of belief formation rather than specific beliefs, can they be treated as patterns of inference, for example from beliefs about the present to beliefs about the future? Represented as a universal generalization, a non-deductive pattern of inference such as abduction is represented as a falsehood, for the relevantly best explanations are not always correct. Nevertheless, we can acquire knowledge abductively because we do not rely on every abduction in relying on one; we sometimes rely on a locally truth-preserving abduction, even though abduction is not globally truth-preserving. The trouble with replacing a pattern of inference by a universal generalization is that it has us rely on all instances of the pattern simultaneously, by relying on the generalization. Even if the universal generalization is replaced by a statement of general tendencies, what we are relying on in a particular case is still inappropriately globalized. Epistemologically, folk 'theories' seem to function more like patterns of inference than like general premises. That conception also solves the earlier problem about the inapplicability of logical operators to folk 'theories', since patterns of inference cannot themselves be negated or made the antecedents of conditionals (although claims of their validity can).

Once such a liberal conception of patterns of inference is allowed, calling a process of belief formation 'inferential' is no longer very informative. Just about any process with a set of beliefs (or suppositions) as input and an expanded set of beliefs (or suppositions) as output counts as 'inferential'. Can we say something more informative about the imaginative exercises by which we judge counterfactuals like (7), whether or not we count them as inferential?

An attractive suggestion is that some kind of simulation is involved: the difficulty is to explain what that means. It is just a hint of an answer to say that in simulation cognitive faculties are run off-line. For example, the cognitive faculties that would be run on-line to evaluate 'She broke her leg' and 'She won the match' as free-standing sentences are run off-line in the evaluation of the counterfactual conditional 'If she had broken her leg she would have won the match'.[3] This suggests that the cognition has a roughly compositional

---

[3] Matters become more complicated if the antecedent or consequent itself contains a counterfactual condition, as in 'If she had murdered the man who would have inherited her money if she had died, she would have been sentenced to life imprisonment if she had been convicted', but the underlying principles are the same.

structure. Our capacity to handle a counterfactual conditional embeds our capacities to handle its antecedent and consequent separately, and our capacity to handle the counterfactual conditional operator involves a general capacity to go from capacities to handle the antecedent and the consequent to a capacity to handle the whole conditional. Here the capacity to handle an expression generally comprises more than mere linguistic understanding of it, since it involves ways of assessing its application that are not built into its meaning. But it virtually never involves a decision procedure that enables us always to determine the truth-values of every sentence in which the expression principally occurs, since we lack such decision procedures. Of course, we can sometimes take shortcuts in evaluating counterfactual conditionals. For instance, we can know that 'If there had been infinitely many stars there would have been infinitely many stars' is true even if we have no idea how to determine whether 'There are infinitely many stars' is true. Nevertheless, the compositional structure just described seems more typical.

How do we advance from capacities to handle the antecedent and the consequent to a capacity to handle the whole conditional? 'Off-line' suggests that the most direct links with perception have been cut, but that vague negative point does not take us far. Perceptual input is crucial to the evaluation of counterfactuals such as (1) and (7).

The best developed simulation theories concern our ability to simulate the mental processes of other agents (or ourselves in other circumstances), putting ourselves in their shoes, as if thinking and deciding on the basis of their beliefs and desires (see for example Davies and Stone 1995, Nichols and Stich 2003). Such cognitive processes may well be relevant to the evaluation of counterfactuals about agents. Moreover, they would involve just the sort of constrained use of the imagination indicated above. How would Mary react if you asked to borrow her car? You could imagine her immediately shooting you, or making you her heir; you could even imagine reacting like that from her point of view, by imagining having sufficiently bizarre beliefs and desires. But you do not. Doing so would not help you determine how she really would react. Presumably, what you do is to hold fixed her actual beliefs and desires (as you take them to be just before the request); you can then imagine the request from her point of view, and think through the scenario from there. Just as with the falling rock, the imaginative exercise is richly informed and disciplined by your sense of what she is like.

How could mental simulation help us evaluate a counterfactual such as (6), which does not concern an agent? Even if you somehow put yourself in the rock's shoes, imagining first-personally being that shape, size and hardness and bouncing down that slope, you would not be simulating the rock's reasoning and decision-making. Thinking of the rock as an agent is no help in determining its counter-factual trajectory. A more natural way to answer the question is by imagining third-personally the rock falling as it would visually appear from your actual present spatial position; you thereby avoid the complex process of adjusting your current visual perspective to the viewpoint of the rock. Is that to simulate the mental states of an observer watching the rock fall from your present position?[4] By itself, that suggestion explains little. For how do we know what to simulate the observer seeing next?

That question is not unanswerable. For we have various propensi-ties to form expectations about what happens next: for example, to project the trajectories of nearby moving bodies into the immediate future (otherwise we could not catch balls). Perhaps we simulate the initial movement of the rock in the absence of the bush, form an expectation as to where it goes next, feed the expected movement back into the simulation as seen by the observer, form a further expectation as to its subsequent movement, feed that back into the simulation, and so on. If our expectations in such matters are app-roximately correct in a range of ordinary cases, such a process is cognitively worthwhile. The very natural laws and causal tendencies our expectations roughly track also help to determine which counter-factual conditionals really hold.

However, talk of simulating the mental states of an observer may suggest that the presence of the observer is part of the content of the simulation. That does not fit our evaluation of counterfactuals. Consider:

(9)   If there had been a tree on this spot a million years ago, nobody would have known.

Even if we visually imagine a tree on this spot a million years ago, we do not automatically reject (9) because we envisage an observer of the tree. We may imagine the tree as having a certain visual appearance from a certain viewpoint, but that is not to say that we imagine it as appearing to someone at that viewpoint. For example, if we imagine the sun as shining from behind that viewpoint, by imagining the tree's shadow stretching back from the tree, we are not obliged to imagine either the observer's shadow stretching towards the tree or

---

[4]   See Goldman 1992: 24, discussed by Nichols, Stich, Leslie and Klein 1996: 53–59.

the observer as perfectly transparent.[5] Nor, when we consider (9), are we asking whether if we had believed that there was a tree on this spot a million years ago, we would have believed that nobody knew.[6] It is better not to regard the simulation as referring to anything specifically *mental* at all.

Of course, for many counterfactuals the relevant expectations are not hardwired into us in the way that those concerning the trajectories of fast-moving objects around us may need to be. Our knowledge that if a British general election had been called in 1948 the Communists would not have won may depend on an off-line use of our capacity to predict political events. Still, where our more sophisticated capacities to predict the future are reliable, so should be corresponding counterfactual judgments. In these cases too, simulating the mental states of an imaginary observer seems unnecessary.

The off-line use of expectation-forming capacities to judge counterfactuals corresponds to the widespread picture of the semantic evaluation of those conditionals as 'rolling back' history to shortly before the time of the antecedent, modifying its course by stipulating the truth of the antecedent and then rolling history forward again according to patterns of development as close as possible to the normal ones to test the truth of the consequent (compare Lewis 1979).

The use of expectation-forming capacities may in effect impose a partial solution to Goodman's problem of cotenability, since they do not operate on information about what happened after the time treated as present. In this respect indicative conditionals are evaluated differently: if I had climbed a mountain yesterday I would remember it today, but if I did climb a mountain yesterday I do not remember it

---

[5]   The question is of course related to Berkeley's claim that we cannot imagine an unseen object. For discussion see Williams 1966, Peacocke 1985 and Currie 1995: 36–37.

[6]   A similar problem arises for what is sometimes called the Ramsey Test for conditionals, on which one simulates belief in the antecedent and asks whether one then believes the consequent. Goldman writes 'When considering the truth value of "If X were the case, then Y would obtain," a reasoner feigns a belief in X and reasons about Y under that pretence" (1992: 24). What Ramsey himself says is that when people 'are fixing their degrees of belief in q given p' they 'are adding p hypothetically to their stock of knowledge and arguing on that basis about q' (1978: 143), but he specifically warns that 'the degree of belief in q given p' does not mean the degree of belief 'which the subject would have in q if he knew p, or that which he ought to have' (1978: 82; variables interchanged). Conditional probabilities bear more directly on indicative than on counterfactual conditionals.

today. The known fact that I do not remember climbing a mountain yesterday is retained under the indicative but not the counterfactual supposition.

Our off-line use of expectation-forming capacities to unroll a counterfactual history from the imagined initial conditions does not explain why we imagine the initial conditions in one way rather than another – for instance, why we do not imagine a wall in place of the bush. Very often, no alternative occurs to us, but that does not mean that the way we go adds nothing to the given antecedent. We seem to have a prereflective tendency to minimum alteration in imagining counterfactual alternatives to actuality, reminiscent of the role that similarity between possible worlds plays in the Lewis-Stalnaker semantics.

Of course, not all counterfactual conditionals can be evaluated by the rolling back method, since the antecedent need not concern a particular time: in evaluating the claim that space-time has ten dimensions, a scientist can sensibly ask whether if it were true the actually observed phenomena would have occurred. Explicit reasoning may play a much larger role in the evaluation of such conditionals.

Reasoning and prediction do not exhaust our capacity to evaluate counterfactuals. If twelve people had come to the party, would it have been a large party? To answer, one does not imagine a party of twelve people and then predict what would happen next. The question is whether twelve people would have constituted a large party, not whether they would have caused one. Nor is the process of answering best conceived as purely inferential, if one has no special antecedent beliefs as to how many people constitute a large party, any more than the judgment whether the party is large is purely inferential when made at the party. Rather, in both cases one must make a new judgment, even though it is informed by what one already believes or imagines about the party. To call the new judgment 'inferential' simply because it is not made independently of all the thinker's prior beliefs or suppositions is to stretch the term 'inferential' beyond its useful span. At any rate, the judgment cannot be derived from the prior beliefs or suppositions purely by the application of general rules of inference. For example, even if you have the prior belief that a party is large if and only if it is larger than the average size of a party, in order to apply it to the case at hand you also need to have a belief as to what the average size of a party is; if you have no prior belief as to that, and must form one by inference, an implausible regress threatens, for you do not have the statistics of parties in your head. Similarly, if you try to judge whether this party is large by projecting inductively from previous judgments as to whether parties were large, that only pushes the question back to how those previous judgments were made.

In general, our capacity to evaluate counterfactuals recruits *all* our cognitive capacities to evaluate sentences. For it can be shown that any sentence whatsoever is equivalent to a counterfactual conditional, for example, to one with that sentence as the consequent and a tautology as the antecedent. Thus, *modulo* the recognition of this elementary equivalence, any cognitive work needed to evaluate the original sentence is also needed to evaluate the counterfactual conditional.

We can schematize the process of evaluating a counterfactual conditional thus: one imaginatively supposes the antecedent and develops the supposition, adding further judgments within the supposition by reasoning, off-line predictive mechanisms and other off-line judgments. All of one's background knowledge and belief is available from within the scope of the supposition as a description of one's actual circumstances for the purposes of comparison with the counterfactual circumstances (in this respect the development differs from that of the antecedent of an indicative conditional). Some but not all of one's background knowledge and belief is also available within the scope of the supposition as a description of the counterfactual circumstances, according to complex criteria (the problem of cotenability). To a first approximation: one asserts the counterfactual conditional if and only if the development eventually leads one to add the consequent.

An over-simplification in that account is that one develops the initial supposition only once. In fact, if one finds various different ways of imagining the antecedent equally good, one may try developing several of them, to test whether they all yield the consequent. For example, if in considering (9) one initially imagines a palm tree, one does not immediately judge that if there had been a tree on this spot a million years ago it would have been a palm tree, because one knows that one can equally easily imagine a fir tree. One repeats the thought experiment. Robustness in the result under such minor perturbations supports a higher degree of confidence.

What happens if the counterfactual development of the antecedent does not robustly yield the consequent? We do not always deny the counterfactual, for several reasons. First, if the consequent has not emerged after a given period of development the question remains whether it will emerge in the course of further development, for lines of reasoning can be continued indefinitely from any given premise. To reach a negative conclusion, one must in effect judge that if the consequent were ever going to emerge it would have done so by now. For example, one may have been smoothly fleshing out a scenario incompatible with the consequent with no hint of difficulty. Second, even if one is confident that the consequent will not robustly emerge from the development, one may suspect that the reason is one's ignorance of relevant background conditions rather than the lack of a counterfactual connection between the antecedent and the consequent ('If I were to follow that path, it would lead me out of the forest'). Thus one may remain agnostic over the counterfactual.

The case for denying the counterfactual is usually strongest when the counterfactual development of the antecedent robustly yields the negation of the consequent. Then one asserts the opposite counterfactual, with the same antecedent and the negated consequent. The default is to deny a counterfactual if one asserts the opposite counterfactual, for example moving from 'If she had broken her leg she would have failed to win the match' to 'It is not the case that if she had broken her leg she would have won the match'. The move is defeasible; sometimes one must accept opposite counterfactuals together. For example, deductive closure generates both 'If she had both won and failed to win the match she would have won the match' and 'If she had both won and failed to win the match she would have failed to win the match'. Normally, if the counterfactual development of the antecedent robustly yields the negation of the consequent and robustly fails to yield the consequent itself then one denies the original counterfactual, but even this connection is defeasible, since one may still suspect that the original consequent (as well as its negation) would robustly emerge given more complex reasoning or further background information.

Sometimes a counterfactual antecedent is manifestly neutral between contradictory consequents: consider 'If the coin had been tossed it would have come up heads' and 'If the coin had been tossed it would have come up tails'. In such cases one will clearly never be in a position to assert one conditional, and thus will never be in a position to use it as a basis for denying the opposite conditional.

The epistemological asymmetry between asserting and denying a counterfactual conditional resembles an epistemological asymmetry in practice between asserting and denying many existential claims. If I find snakes in Iceland, without too much fuss I can assert that there are snakes in Iceland. If I fail to find snakes in Iceland, I cannot deny that there are snakes in Iceland without some implicit or explicit assessment of the thoroughness of my search: if there were snakes in Iceland, would I have found some by now? But we are capable of making such assessments, and sometimes are in a position to deny such existential claims. Similarly, if I find a counterfactual connection between the antecedent and the consequent (my counter-factual development of the former robustly yields the latter) without too much fuss I can assert the counterfactual. If I fail to find a counterfactual connection between the antecedent and the consequent (my counterfactual development of the former does not robustly yield the latter), I cannot deny the counterfactual without some implicit or explicit assessment of the thoroughness of my search: if there were a counterfactual connection, would I have found it by now? But we are capable of making such assessments, and sometimes are in a position to deny counterfactual conditionals.

Despite its discipline, our imaginative evaluation of counterfactual conditionals is manifestly fallible. We can easily misjudge their truth-values, through background ignorance or error, and distortions of judgment. But such fallibility is the common lot of human cognition. Our use of the imagination in evaluating counterfactuals is practically indispensable. Rather than cave in to scepticism, we should admit that our methods sometimes yield knowledge of counterfactuals.

Some counterfactual conditions look like paradigms of *a priori* knowability: for example (8), whose consequent is a straightforward deductive consequence of its antecedent. Others look like paradigms of what can be known only *a posteriori*: for example, that if I had searched in my pocket five minutes ago I would have found a coin. But those are easy cases.

Standard discussions of the *a priori* distinguish between two roles that experience plays in cognition, one *evidential*, one *enabling*. Experience is held to play an evidential role in my visual knowledge that this shirt is green, but a merely enabling role in my knowledge that all green things are coloured: I needed it only to acquire the concepts *green* and *coloured*, without which I could not even raise the question whether all green things are coloured. Knowing *a priori* is supposed to be incompatible with an evidential role for experience, or at least with an evidential role for sense experience, so my knowledge that this shirt is green is not *a priori*. By contrast, knowing *a priori* is supposed to be compatible with an enabling role for experience, so my knowledge that all green things are coloured can still be *a priori*. However, in our imagination-based knowledge of counterfactuals, sense experience can play a role that is neither strictly evidential nor purely enabling. For, even without surviving as part of our total evidence, it can mould our habits of imagination and judgment in ways that go far beyond a merely enabling role.

Here is an example. I acquire the words 'inch' and 'centimetre' independently of each other. Through sense experience, I learn to make naked eye judgments of distances in inches or centimetres with moderate reliability. When things go well, such judgments amount to knowledge: *a posteriori* knowledge, of course. For example, I know *a posteriori* that two marks in front of me are at most two inches apart. Now I deploy the same faculty off-line to make a counterfactual judgment:

(10)   If two marks had been nine inches apart, they would have been at least nineteen centimetres apart.

In judging (10), I do not use a conversion ratio between inches and centimetres to make a calculation. In the example I know no such ratio. Rather, I visually imagine two marks nine inches apart, and use my ability to judge distances in centimetres visually off-line to judge under the counterfactual supposition that they are at least nineteen centimetres apart. With this large margin for error, my judgment is reliable. Thus I know (10). Do I know it *a priori* or *a posteriori*? Sense experience plays no direct evidential role in my judgment. I do not consciously or unconsciously recall memories of distances encountered in perception, nor do I deduce (10) from general premises I have inductively or abductively gathered from experience: we noted above obstacles to assimilating such patterns of counterfactual judgment to the use of general premises. Nevertheless, the causal role of past sense experience in my judgment of (10) far exceeds enabling me to grasp the concepts relevant to (10). Someone could easily have enough sense experience to understand (10) without being reliable enough in their judgments of distance to know (10). Nor is the role of past experience in the judgment of (10) purely enabling in some other way, for example by acquainting me with a logical argument for (10). It is more directly implicated than that. Whether my belief in (10) constitutes knowledge is highly sensitive to the accuracy or otherwise of the empirical information about lengths (in each unit) on which I relied when calibrating my judgments of length (in each unit). I know (10) only if my off-line application of the concepts of an inch and a centimetre was sufficiently skilful. My possession of the appropriate skills depends constitutively, not just causally, on past experience for the calibration of my judgments of length in those units. If the calibration is correct by a lucky accident, despite massive errors in the relevant past beliefs about length, I lack the required skill.[7]

If we knew counterfactual conditionals by purely *a priori* inference from the antecedent and background premises to the conclusion, our

---

[7]   Yablo 2002 has a related discussion of the concept *oval*.

knowledge might count as *a priori* if we knew all the background pre-mises *a priori*, and otherwise as *a posteriori*. However, it was argued above that if the process is inferential at all, the relevant inferences are themselves of just the kind for which past experience plays a role that is neither purely enabling nor strictly evidential, so the infer-ential picture does not resolve the issue.

If we classify my knowledge of (10) in the envisaged circumstances as *a priori*, because sense experience plays no strictly evidential role, the danger is that far too much will count as *a priori*. Long-forgotten experience can mould my judgment in many ways without playing a direct evidential role, for example by conditioning me into patterns of expectation which are called on in my assessment of ordinary coun-terfactual conditionals. But if we classify my knowledge of (10) as *a posteriori*, because experience plays more than a purely enabling role, that may apply to many philosophically significant judgments too. For example:

(11)   If you had been morally obliged to give the money, you would have been able to give it.

If we know (11), our way of knowing it is similar to our way of knowing (10). Knowledge of truths like (11) is usually regarded as *a priori*, even by those who accept the category of the necessary *a pos-teriori*. The experiences through which we learned to distinguish in practice between the obligatory and the non-obligatory and between ability and inability play no strictly evidential role in our knowledge of (11). Nevertheless, their role may be more than purely enabling. Why should not subtle differences between two courses of experience, each of which sufficed for coming to under-stand (11), make for differences in how test cases are processed, just large enough to tip honest judgments in opposite directions? Whether knowledge of (11) is available to one may thus be highly sen-sitive to personal circumstances. Such individual differences in the skill with which concepts are applied depend constitutively, not just causally, on past experience, for the skillfulness of a performance depends constitutively on its causal origins.

In a similar way, past experience of spatial and temporal properties may play a role in skilful mathematical 'intuition' that is not directly evidential but far exceeds what is needed to acquire the relevant mathematical concepts. The role may be more than heuristic, con-cerning the context of justification as well as the context of discovery. Even the combinatorial skills required for competent assessment of standard set-theoretic axioms may involve off-line applications of perceptual and motor skills, whose capacity to generate knowledge constitutively depends on their honing through past experience that plays no evidential role in the assessment of the axioms.

If the preceding picture is on the right lines, should we conclude that modal knowledge is *a posteriori*? Not if that suggests that (11) is an inductive or abductive conclusion from perceptual data. In such cases, the question '*A priori* or *a posteriori*?' is too crude to be of much epistemological use. The point is not that we cannot draw a line somewhere with traditional paradigms of the *a priori* on one side and traditional paradigms of the *a posteriori* on the other. Surely we can; the point is that doing so yields little insight. The distinction is handy enough for a rough initial description of epistemic phenomena; it is out of place in a deeper theoretical analysis, because it obscures more significant epistemic patterns. We may acknowledge an extensive category of *armchair knowledge*, in the sense of knowledge in which experience plays no strictly evidential role, while remembering that such knowledge may not fit the stereotype of the *a priori*, because the contribution of experience was far more than enabling. For example, it should be no surprise if we turn out to have armchair knowledge of truths about the external environment.[8]

New College, Oxford

Bibliography

Anderson, A. R. (1951) "A note on subjunctive and counterfactual conditionals", *Analysis* **12**, 35–8.

Byrne, R. M. J. (2005) *The Rational Imagination: How People Create Alternatives to Reality*. Cambridge, Mass.: MIT Press.

Chalmers, D. J. (2006) "The foundations of two-dimensional semantics", in M. García-Carpintero and J. Macià, eds., *Two-Dimensional Semantics*, Oxford: Clarendon Press.

Collins, J., Hall, N., and Paul, L. A. (2004) *Causation and Counterfactuals*. Cambridge, MA: M.I.T. Press.

[8]   This problem for the *a priori*/*a posteriori* distinction undermines arguments for the incompatibility of semantic externalism with our privileged access to our own mental states that appeal to the supposed absurdity of *a priori* knowledge of contingent features of the external environment (McKinsey 1991). It also renders problematic attempts to explain the first dimension of two-dimensional semantics in terms of *a priori* knowability, as in Chalmers 2006. Substituting talk of rational reflection for talk of the *a priori* does not help, since it raises parallel questions.

Currie, G. (1995) "Visual imagery as the simulation of vision", *Mind and Language* **10**, 17–44.

Davies M. and Stone T. (eds.) (1995) *Mental Simulation: Evaluation and Applications*. Oxford: Blackwell.

Edgington, D. (2003) "Counterfactuals and the Benefit of Hindsight", *Causation and Counterfactuals*, (eds.) P. Dowe and P. Noordhof. London: Routledge.

Evans, J. St. B. T., and Over, D. E. (2004) *If*. Oxford: Oxford University Press.

Goldman, A. (1992) "Empathy, mind and morals", *Proceedings and Addresses of the American Philosophical Association* **66/3**, 17–41.

Goodman, N. (1954) *Fact, Fiction and Forecast*. London: Athlone Press.

Harris, P. (2000) *The Work of the Imagination*. Oxford: Blackwell.

Jackson, F. (1977) "A causal theory of counterfactuals", *Australasian Journal of Philosophy* **55**, 3–21.

Kahneman, D., and Tversky, A. (1982) "The simulation heuristic", in *Judgement under Uncertainty*, (eds.) D. Kahneman, P. Slovic and A. Tversky. Cambridge: Cambridge University Press.

Lewis, D. K. (1973) "Causation", *Journal of Philosophy* **70**, 556–67.

———— (1979) "Counterfactual dependence and time's arrow", *Noûs* **13**, 455–476.

———— (1986) *Counterfactuals*, revised edn. Cambridge, Mass.: Harvard University Press.

McKinsey, M. (1991) "Anti-individualism and privileged access", *Analysis* **51**, 9–16.

Nichols, S., and Stich, S. P. (2003) *Mindreading: An Integrated Account of Pretence, Self-Awareness, and Understanding of Other Minds*. Oxford: Clarendon Press.

Nichols, S., Stich, S. P., Leslie, A., and Klein, D. (1996) "Varieties of off-line simulation", in *Theories of Theories of Mind*, (eds.) P. Carruthers and P. K. Smith. Cambridge, Cambridge University Press.

Peacocke, C. A. B. (1985) "Imagination, experience and possibility", in *Essays on Berkeley: A Tercentennial Celebration*, (eds.) J. Foster and H. Robinson. Oxford: Clarendon Press.

Ramsey, F. P. (1978) *Foundations: Essays in Philosophy, Logic, Mathematics and Economics*, (ed.) D. H. Mellor. London: Routledge & Kegan Paul.

Roese, N. J., and Olson, J. (1993) "The structure of counterfactual thought", *Personality and Social Psychology Bulletin* **19**, 312–19.

————— (1995) "Functions of counterfactual thinking", in *What Might Have Been: The Social Psychology of Counterfactual Thinking*, (eds.) N. J. Roese and J. M. Olson. Mahwah, NJ: Erlbaum.

Stalnaker, R. (1968) "A theory of conditionals", in *American Philosophical Quarterly Monographs* **2** (*Studies in Logical Theory*), 98–112.

Williams, B. (1966) "Imagination and the self", *Proceedings of the British Academy* **52**, 105–124.

Williamson, T. (2007) *The Philosophy of Philosophy*. Oxford: Blackwell.

Yablo, S. (2002) "Coulda, woulda, shoulda", in *Conceivability and Possibility*, (eds.) T. S. Gendler and J. Hawthorne. Oxford: Clarendon Press.

How I Know I'm Not a Brain in a Vat*

JOSÉ L. ZALABARDO

1. Introduction

The problem of scepticism, as it figures in contemporary epistemology, takes the form of a series of arguments for the conclusion that we don't have much of the knowledge that we think we have. Some of the most prominent arguments for this conclusion take as their starting point *sceptical hypotheses*. Perhaps the most famous of these is Descartes' evil demon hypothesis, according to which

> [. . .] some malicious demon of the utmost power and cunning has employed all his energies in order to deceive me. [. . .] the sky, the air, the earth, colours, shapes, sounds and all external things are merely delusions of dreams that he has devised to ensnare my judgement.[1]

Hilary Putnam's brain-in-a-vat hypothesis (BIV) offers a contemporary variation on the Cartesian theme:

> [. . .] imagine that a human being (you can imagine this to be yourself) has been subjected to an operation by an evil scientist. The person's brain (your brain) has been removed from the body and placed in a vat of nutrients which keeps the brain alive. The nerve endings have been connected to a super-scientific computer which causes the person whose brain it is to have the illusion that everything is perfectly normal. There seem to be people, objects, the sky, etc; but really all the person (you) is experiencing is the result of electronic impulses travelling from the computer to the nerve endings.[2]

*   I have presented versions of this paper at the Arché Centre of the University of St Andrews, the Cambridge Moral Sciences Club, the Royal Institute of Philosophy 2006–7 lecture series and the conference organised by the Instituto de Investigaciones Filosóficas in Mexico to celebrate the 40th anniversary of the journal *Crítica*. I am grateful to these audiences, especially to Mike Martin. Support from the British Academy to attend the *Crítica* conference is gratefully acknowledged.

[1]   R. Descartes 1984: 15.
[2]   H. Putnam 1981: 5–6.

doi:10.1017/S1358246109000071

José L. Zalabardo

There are several ways in which sceptical hypotheses can be used in an argument for the sceptical conclusion that I have very little knowledge. One that has received a good deal of attention in recent debates seeks to draw a conclusion to this effect from two thoughts concerning sceptical hypotheses, namely, that we don't know that they don't obtain and that if we don't know this then there is a lot else that we don't know either.[3] I shall refer to this line of reasoning as the *canonical sceptical argument*.[4]

We can present the structure of the argument in a typical instance using the brain-in-a-vat hypothesis:

P1: I don't know not-BIV.
P2: If I don't know not-BIV, I don't know that I have a broken fingernail.

Therefore:

C: I don't know that I have a broken fingernail.

It is unquestionable that the premises of the canonical argument entail its conclusion. Hence resisting the conclusion would seem to require rejecting at least one of the premises. Both strategies enjoy support.

Rejecting the second premise is the strategy for resisting the canonical argument endorsed by Robert Nozick and Fred Dretske.[5] One serious obstacle to their approach is the fact that in many instances of the canonical argument the second premise follows from the principle that knowledge is closed under known entailment:

Closure: If S knows that p and S knows that p entails q, then S knows that q.

Clearly P2 follows from Closure, since I know that my having a broken fingernail entails not-BIV. Hence pursuing the Dretske/Nozick approach to the canonical argument requires rejecting Closure.[6] Both authors have argued that this move can be independently motivated, but many contemporary epistemologists disagree.

---

[3]   For an alternative approach to the use of sceptical hypotheses in sceptical arguments see A. Brueckner 1994.
[4]   Cf. Ibid., 827.
[5]   Cf. F. Dretske 1970, R. Nozick 1981: Ch. 3.
[6]   As DeRose has observed, in some instances of the canonical argument the second premise seems compelling even though it doesn't follow from Closure – because the proposition that figures in the consequent is compatible with the sceptical hypothesis. See K. DeRose 1995: 32 fn. See also J. Pryor 2000: 522.

On the contrary, they regard the rejection of Closure as too high a price to pay for victory over the sceptic — at least if other strategies are available.

The alternative strategy is to reject the first premise of the canonical argument, arguing in each case that we know that the sceptical hypotheses don't obtain, or, at least, that the sceptic hasn't shown that we don't. My main goal in this paper is to defend a version of this line of thought.

2. DeRose and the Canonical Argument

I want to introduce my proposal by looking at the strategy for dealing with the canonical sceptical argument advanced by Keith DeRose. DeRose is of course best known for his contextualist account of the semantics of sentences ascribing or denying knowledge — the view that their content varies with the context in which they are uttered.[7] But in his treatment of the canonical argument he deploys several interesting ideas that don't depend on his contextualist views. The strategy that I am going to put forward will be similar in important respects to the position that would result if DeRose's ideas were purged of their contextualist aspects.

Let me start by introducing some central features of DeRose's position. As I've just mentioned, DeRose believes that the content of sentences ascribing or denying knowledge depends on the context in which they are uttered. The way in which context affects the content of these sentences is, according to DeRose, by determining how strong an epistemic position you need to be in in order to make a knowledge-ascribing sentence true. While in everyday contexts the standards are relatively undemanding, in contexts in which sceptical hypotheses are under discussion they are much more exacting. Here is DeRose's explanation of the crucial notion of the strength of one's epistemic position, in terms of the possible-world idiom:

> An important component of being in a strong epistemic position with respect to P is to have one's belief as to whether P is true match the fact of the matter as to whether P is true, not only in the actual world, but also at the worlds sufficiently close to the actual world. That is, one's belief should not only be true, but should be non-accidentally true, where this requires one's belief as to whether P is true to match the fact of the matter at

---

[7] Cf. K. DeRose 1995, K. DeRose 1999.

nearby worlds. The further away one can get from the actual world, while still having it be the case that one's belief matches the fact at worlds that far away and closer, the stronger the position one is in with respect to P.[8]

Knowledge, according to DeRose, requires a certain level of strength in your epistemic position with respect to the known proposition. Thus, in terms of DeRose's construal of the strength of one's epistemic position, it requires that your belief tracks the truth in a certain sphere of possible worlds, centred in the actual world, to which he refers as the *sphere of epistemically relevant worlds*.[9]

Now we can provide a precise characterisation of how context affects the content of sentences ascribing or denying knowledge on DeRose's position. Context, according to DeRose, determines how far the sphere of epistemically relevant words extends – how far into counterfactual space your belief needs to track the truth in order to count as knowledge.

In everyday contexts, the sphere of epistemically relevant words doesn't extend very far. In order to make a knowledge-ascribing sentence true, when uttered in such a context, your belief would only have to track the truth in a relatively reduced range of worlds. And both my belief that I have a broken fingernail and my belief that I am not a brain in a vat satisfy this requirement. This fact provides the key to DeRose's rejection of the challenge to our everyday knowledge claims posed by the canonical argument.

DeRose's semantics for the verb 'to know' get in the way of a straightforward presentation of his anti-sceptical strategy.[10] In order to overcome this difficulty, I propose to introduce a context-insensitive neologism to express how, according to DeRose, a subject S has to be related to a proposition p in order to make 'S knows that p' true when uttered in an everyday context. Thus, let 'DR(E)-knows' be a binary predicate that is true of a subject S and a proposition p just in case S's belief that p tracks the truth of p in the sphere of epistemically relevant worlds in force in everyday contexts.

Now, in order to challenge the claim that I would express in an everyday context with the sentence 'I know that I have a broken fingernail', the sceptic would have to establish the following conclusion:

CE: JZ doesn't DR(E)-know that he has a broken fingernail.

[8]   K. DeRose 1995: 34.
[9]   Ibid. 37.
[10] See, in this connection, Ibid. 40 fn.

And to establish this conclusion with the canonical sceptical argument, she would have to invoke the following premises:

P1E: JZ doesn't DR(E)-know not-BIV.

P2E: If JZ doesn't DR(E)-know not-BIV, then he doesn't DR(E)-know that he has a broken fingernail.

DeRose's treatment of this argument is an instance of the strategy that I want to recommend. He feels entitled to resist the conclusion of this valid argument because, even though he believes the second premise to be true, he thinks that the first premise is false.[11] In the sphere of epistemically relevant worlds in force in everyday contexts, my belief in not-BIV does track the truth.

Once we have defused the argument for CE in this way, we have removed the pressure that the canonical argument placed on our everyday knowledge claims. And with this, DeRose thinks, the main job of refuting the sceptic can be brought to an end. For the reason why sceptical arguments pose a serious problem is that they threaten to show,

> [...] not only that we fail to meet very high requirements for knowledge of interest only to misguided philosophers seeking absolute certainty, but that we don't meet even the truth conditions of ordinary, out-on-the-street knowledge attributions. They thus threaten to establish the startling result that we never, or almost never, truthfully ascribe knowledge to ourselves or to other mere mortals.[12]

I want to highlight the fact that in this defence of our everyday claims to knowledge from the threat of the canonical argument no role is played by DeRose's contextualism. The strategy would still be available to someone who thought that the sphere of epistemically relevant worlds is fixed for every context – that an utterance of 'S knows that p', in any context, is true just in case S DR(E)-knows that p.[13]

Nevertheless, contextualism still has an important role to play in DeRose's overall treatment of the canonical argument. For the goal of his strategy is twofold: "To safeguard ordinary claims to know while at the same time explaining the persuasiveness of the skeptical

---

[11]   "Thus, on our solution, we do know, for instance, that we are not BIVs, according to ordinary standards of knowledge" (Ibid. 39).

[12]   Ibid. 4. See also his remarks on the timid sceptic on 5–6.

[13]   In a recent paper, DeRose has spelt out the connections between his position and non-contextualist views that reject the first premise of the canonical argument. See K. DeRose 2004.

José L. Zalabardo

arguments [...]".[14] As we have seen, contextualism has no role to play in the first of these tasks. It is in the second task — explaining the persuasiveness of sceptical arguments — that DeRose's strategy makes use of contextualism. Given that he is proposing to resist the canonical argument by rejecting the first premise, naturally his main challenge in discharging the second task is to explain what makes this premise so appealing, "to explain what it is about sceptical hypotheses that makes it so plausible to suppose that we don't know that they're false".[15]

The crucial point here is that on DeRose's account, when the sceptic utters 'JZ doesn't know not-BIV', she immediately generates a conversational context in which the extent of the sphere of epistemically relevant worlds is radically expanded — to include worlds in which BIV is true.[16] But in those worlds I believe not-BIV — it is a salient feature of sceptical hypotheses that if they were true I would still believe them to be false. Hence, my belief in not-BIV doesn't track the truth in the sphere of epistemically relevant worlds that is in force in this context. Therefore, when the sceptic utters 'JZ doesn't know not-BIV' she is speaking the truth. Furthermore, my utterance of 'I know not-BIV' would have the same effect on the conversational context. This is DeRose's explanation of why we find the first premise of the canonical argument so plausible:

> [...] we are able to explain its plausibility [...] by means of the fact that the high standards at which (1) [the first premise of the canonical argument] is true are precisely the standards that an assertion or denial of it put into play. Since attempts to assert (1) are bound to result in truth, and attempts to deny it are destined to produce falsehood, it is no surprise that we find it so plausible.[17]

Notice that the truth that is expressed by an utterance of 'JZ doesn't know not-BIV' is not the proposition that would enable the sceptic to establish CE with the canonical argument. Let me introduce one more binary predicate, 'DR(H)-knows', true of a subject S and a proposition p just in case S's belief that p tracks the truth of p in the sphere of epistemically relevant worlds in force when

---

[14]   K. DeRose 1995: 6.

[15]   Ibid. 17.

[16]   DeRose's ingenious account of how this expansion of the sphere of epistemically relevant worlds comes about is his Rule of Sensitivity. See Ibid. 36.

[17]   Ibid. 40.

my knowledge of not-BIV is asserted or denied. Then, the sceptic's utterance of 'JZ doesn't know not-BIV' expresses the proposition:

P1H: JZ doesn't DR(H)-know not-BIV.

To get from here to CE, the sceptic would need, as an additional premise, the proposition:

P2HE: If JZ doesn't DR(H)-know not-BIV, then he doesn't DR(E)-know that he has a broken fingernail.

But P2HE is false. Even though my belief in not-BIV doesn't track the truth in the sphere of epistemically relevant worlds instituted by discussion of my knowledge of not-BIV, my belief that I have a broken fingernail tracks the truth in the sphere of epistemically relevant worlds in force in everyday contexts.

The (true) proposition that would be expressed by uttering in the sceptical context the sentence 'If JZ doesn't know not-BIV, then he doesn't know that he has a broken fingernail' is rather:

P2H: If JZ doesn't DR(H)-know not-BIV, then he doesn't DR(H)-know that he has a broken fingernail.

From this, the sceptic can derive

CH: JZ doesn't DR(H)-know that he has a broken fingernail.

This is the true proposition that would be expressed by an utterance in the sceptical context of the sentence 'JZ doesn't know that he has a broken fingernail'. Hence, when the sceptic asserts her conclusion, she speaks the truth, but not the putative truth (CE) that she was aiming to establish, but the much less disturbing truth that, with respect to the state of my fingernail, I fail to meet "very high requirements for knowledge of interest only to misguided philosophers seeking absolute certainty". In sum, DeRose's explanation of the plausibility of the canonical argument doesn't reinstate the threat to our everyday knowledge claims.

Now, I am what DeRose calls a nonsceptical invariantist.[18] I think that utterances of 'S knows that p' express the same proposition in all contexts, and that this proposition is quite close to the proposition that DeRose thinks they express in everyday contexts. This means that I'll be able to join DeRose in vindicating our everyday knowledge claims in the face of the challenge of the canonical argument by rejecting its first premise. I know not-BIV, or at least the sceptic hasn't shown that I don't. My goal in the remainder of this paper is to

---

[18]   Cf. K. DeRose 1999: 192.

José L. Zalabardo

spell out the features of the concept of knowledge that enable us to adopt this position.

The price I have to pay for rejecting DeRose's contextualist semantics for the verb 'to know' is that I won't be able to avail myself of his explanation of the intuitive plausibility of the canonical argument. I face the challenge that DeRose poses for straightforward (i.e. non-contextualist) solutions to the problem:

> To succeed, a straightforward solution must explain what leads our intuitions astray with respect to the unlucky member of the triad [the premises of the canonical argument and the negation of its conclusion] which that solution denies.[19]

In my case, the challenge consists in explaining our intuitive reluctance to claim what I hold to be true – that we know that sceptical hypotheses don't obtain. This is a challenge that I accept, but the task of meeting it will be left for another occasion.

3. The Risk of Error

A very interesting aspect of DeRose's position is a contrast between the way I DR(E)-know that I have a broken fingernail and the way I DR(E)-know not-BIV. I DR(E)-know the former by virtue of the fact that my belief that I have a broken fingernail is *sensitive* to the truth of the proposition that I have a broken fingernail – i.e. if I didn't have a broken fingernail I wouldn't believe that I do. By contrast, for DR(E)-knowledge of not-BIV, sensitivity is not needed. I DR(E)-know this by virtue of the fact that the sphere of epistemically relevant worlds contains only worlds in which not-BIV is true and I believe it. My belief is not sensitive, but the nearest worlds in which its insensitivity is manifested (BIV worlds) lie outside the sphere of epistemically relevant worlds.

We have then that, on DeRose's position, what it takes to DR(E)-know a proposition depends on whether or not the sphere of epistemically relevant worlds contains worlds in which the proposition is false. If, on the one hand, there are no such worlds, it would be enough for you to believe the proposition in every world in this sphere. If, on the other hand, there are such worlds, your belief will need to be sensitive.

I think that this comes very close to adequately grasping an important intuition about knowledge – that *a true belief won't have the status*

---

[19]   K. DeRose 1995: 42.

of knowledge if there is a substantial and uncontrolled risk of the belief being in error. I shall refer to this as the *Risk of Error (ROE) constraint*.

The first feature of the ROE constraint that I want to highlight is the fact that what it takes to satisfy it depends on whether a substantial risk of error exists. If, on the one hand, there is no substantial risk of a belief being in error, the constraint is immediately satisfied. This corresponds, in DeRose's account of knowledge in everyday contexts, to the fact that when a belief is true throughout the sphere of epistemically relevant worlds, it doesn't need to be sensitive in order to have the status of knowledge. If, on the other hand, a substantial risk of error exists, satisfying the constraint requires bringing the risk under control. This is achieved, in DeRose's picture, when the belief is sensitive. My belief that not-BIV satisfies the ROE constraint in the first of these ways, and my belief that I have a broken fingernail in the second. In this section I want to offer a construal of the ROE constraint that will be similar in outline to DeRose's account of the strength of one's epistemic position required for knowledge in everyday contexts, but will depart from DeRose's position in a few important respects.

Let me start by fixing the sphere of epistemically relevant worlds for all contexts roughly at the level at which DeRose would place it for everyday contexts. I shall refer to it as the *Relevant Sphere*. It contains worlds in which my fingernail is not broken, worlds in which I have no hands, etc. but not worlds in which I am a brain in a vat or a victim of a Cartesian evil demon. Notice, though, that the Relevant Sphere doesn't exclude demon and BIV worlds by definition. It excludes them only if they are indeed as distant from the actual world as we think they are. Clearly, this description of the Relevant Sphere leaves a huge scope for borderline cases, and this feature will be inherited by the constraint on knowledge that I am going to formulate in terms of it.

Whether your belief satisfies the ROE constraint will depend exclusively on what happens within the Relevant Sphere. This reflects the fact that satisfying the constraint requires bringing the risk of error under control only when it is substantial. According to this approach, in order to determine whether a belief satisfies the ROE constraint, the first factor that we'll need to consider is whether a substantial risk of error exists. A substantial risk of error will exist if, and only if, the Relevant Sphere contains worlds in which the belief is false. In cases in which there is no substantial risk of error – i.e. when the Relevant Sphere contains no worlds in which your belief is false, the belief will satisfies the ROE constraint by default. No additional condition will have to be met for the constraint to be satisfied.

José L. Zalabardo

Notice that the ROE constraint is even less demanding in these cases than DeRose's notion of an epistemic position strong enough for knowledge in everyday contexts. For, according to DeRose, even if the Relevant Sphere contains only worlds in which your belief is true, your epistemic position will fail to be strong (to the degree under discussion) if in some of those worlds you don't have the belief (or at least if you believe its negation).[20] No such restriction is imposed by the ROE constraint. If you believe that p, and p is true throughout the Relevant Sphere, then your belief will satisfy the ROE constraint even if in some of these worlds you don't believe that p.

I think that intuition is firmly on the side of permissiveness on this point. If BIV-worlds are indeed as distant as I think they are, then I can't see why the existence of nearby worlds in which I believe that I am a brain in a vat, as a result of, say, brainwashing, or too much philosophy – why the existence of these worlds should pose an obstacle to bestowing on my actual belief in not-BIV the status of knowledge.

This corresponds to a general difference between the conception of error with which DeRose operates and the conception that I propose to treat as relevant. On DeRose's picture, the risk that needs to be kept at bay in order for knowledge to be possible is the risk that your belief as to whether or not p might be in error. Clearly this risk is posed not only by worlds in which you believe that p but p is false, but also by worlds in which you don't believe that p (or you believe that not-p) and p is true. What I am proposing is that what is relevant to whether or not your belief that p has the status of knowledge is the risk that you might erroneously believe that p. Consequently, the risk that you might erroneously fail to believe p, or believe not-p, will be irrelevant to the satisfaction of the ROE constraint.

This feature of my approach will be reflected by the fact that the ROE constraint will abide by the following *Principle of Asymmetry*:

> **PA:** If S believes that p and p is true, satisfaction of the ROE constraint by S's belief that p will not depend on what happens in counterfactual situations in which p is true.[21]

[20]   "Where not-P (here, *I am a BIV*) is quite remote, one can be in a quite strong epistemic position with respect to P merely by believing that P in all the nearby worlds" (Ibid. 35). The point that DeRose is making is that nothing but believing that P in all the nearby worlds is required in these cases for a strong epistemic position, but he seems to be asserting, by implication, that this is a requirement for a strong epistemic position.

[21]   It might clarify matters to think that DeRose's account of an epistemic position sufficiently strong for everyday purposes is related to Nozick's account of knowledge as the ROE constraint is related to the account of

So far we have considered cases in which no substantial risk of error is present. I have argued that in these cases no further condition is required for the satisfaction of the ROE constraint. So if worlds in which sceptical hypotheses are true are as remote as we think they are, i.e. outside the Relevant Sphere, our beliefs to the effect that they are false will satisfy the constraint in this way.

Let me now turn to cases in which a substantial risk of error is present – beliefs that are false somewhere in the Relevant Sphere. When the risk of error is substantial, satisfying the ROE constraint will require bringing the risk under control. One way in which this can be achieved is by being protected against the risk, and a belief will be protected from the risk of error precisely when it is sensitive. If you believe that p and things are such that, if p were false you wouldn't believe that p, then the risk of error posed by non-p worlds in the Relevant Sphere will be kept at bay.

Notice that, in accordance with the Principle of Asymmetry, it is not required, in addition, that S believes that p in nearby situations in which p is true. What S believes in those situations will have no consequences for whether S's belief that p is protected from the risk of error. This aspect of my approach answers to the intuition that S's true belief that p can have the status of knowledge when its sensitivity is due to the fact that S's cognitive devices make belief in p dependent on the satisfaction of a condition q that isn't satisfied in any not-p worlds but also goes unsatisfied in many nearby p-worlds. If, in these circumstances, S believes that p because her cognitive devices have detected the satisfaction of q, there will be nearby p-worlds in which S doesn't believe p.

This way of satisfying the ROE constraint corresponds to the way in which, in DeRose's picture, we achieve a strong epistemic position with respect to the propositions that figure in our everyday knowledge claims. The construal of the ROE constraint that I want to put forward will differ from DeRose's approach in offering an alternative method for bringing the risk of error under control, in addition to being protected against it. My proposal is that the risk will also be under control when the subject has identified adequate evidence in its support.

For the purposes of the ROE constraint, adequate evidence for p is a true proposition q that wouldn't be true if p weren't true. If we say that fact A is *sensitive* to fact B just in case A doesn't obtain in the nearest worlds in which B doesn't obtain, q will provide adequate

---

knowledge that would result if we removed Condition 4 from Nozick's analysis. Cf. R. Nozick 1981: 176–78.

evidence for p when the fact that q is sensitive to the fact that p. If q constitutes adequate evidence for p, S will have identified this evidence when she believes that q and that q is sensitive to p, and these beliefs of hers satisfy the ROE constraint. Clearly, this situation will only effect satisfaction of the ROE constraint by S's belief that p in cases in which this belief doesn't independently satisfy the constraint. When satisfaction of the constraint by S's belief that q and that q is sensitive to p somehow presupposes its satisfaction by S's belief that p, S's belief that p will never come to satisfy the constraint through S's identification of the evidential support provided by q. I shall refer to this form of risk control as *evidential control*.

My proposal is, then, that in cases in which there is a substantial risk of error, the ROE constraint will be satisfied either when the belief is protected from the risk of error by sensitivity, or when the subject has identified adequate evidence for it.

4. Evidence and Sensitivity

One obvious difference between this approach and the account of the strength of one's epistemic position advanced by DeRose is that in DeRose's picture there is no analogue of the evidential method for bringing the risk of error under control. DeRose clearly accepts that one's epistemic position with respect to a proposition can be made strong, to the requisite degree, by identifying evidence for it. Nevertheless he sees no need to mention evidence separately as a source of epistemic strength, because he thinks that these cases are already covered by the stipulation that one's epistemic situation can be made strong by sensitivity.[22] The point that I am attributing to DeRose can be expressed in terms of the following principle linking evidential knowledge and sensitivity:

[22]   Here is a representative passage: "[...] by checking appropriately independent sources, I could get myself into a position in which I seemingly *would* know that the newspaper isn't mistaken about whether the Bulls won last night. But the checks that would seemingly allow this knowledge would also make it seem that if the paper were mistaken, I would *not* believe it wasn't." (K. DeRose 1995: 25). Nozick made a similar claim in his discussion of strong evidence, although Nozick's version of the thought is rendered less vulnerable by the fact that he restricts it to cases in which you believe h *on the basis of* strong evidence e, where this requires that your belief that h "depends upon (and varies with)" your belief that e. See R. Nozick 1981: 249. And, as we are about to see, Nozick, unlike DeRose, explicitly endorses the controversial consequences of his claim.

ES: S's identification of adequate evidence for p bestows on her true belief that p the status of knowledge just in case it renders the belief sensitive.

I want to defend my proposal that evidence should be treated separately by raising some problems concerning ES.

The source of the problems is that, as it stands, the principle has obvious counterexamples. One is provided by Nozick's grandmother case: "A grandmother sees her grandson is well when he comes to visit; but if he were sick or dead, others would tell her he was well to spare her upset".[23] While we would want to say that the grandmother knows that her grandson is well as a result of the evidence that she identifies during his visit, her belief is not sensitive. The grandmother's belief that her grandson is well is a counterexample to ES.

The strategy that Nozick puts forward to deal with this difficulty, for which DeRose expresses guarded support, is to relativise the notion of sensitivity to the method employed for forming the belief. The grandmother believes that her grandson is well in the nearest worlds in which he isn't well, but in these worlds her belief is not formed with the same method with which she forms it in the actual world. Her belief that her grandson is well can still have the status of knowledge if she doesn't have it in the nearest worlds in which her grandson is not well *and she arrives at her belief whether or not he is well with the method that she used in actuality to form her belief that he is well.*

Simplifying somewhat Nozick's presentation, we can introduce the following method-relative notion of sensitivity:

S's belief that p is *M-sensitive* just in case, if p were false and S were to arrive at a belief whether or not p with the method she actually used for forming her belief that p, she wouldn't believe that p.

We can now use this notion to formulate a version of the Evidence-Sensitivity Principle that addresses the difficulty:

ES*: S's identification of adequate evidence for p bestows on her true belief that p the status of knowledge just in case it renders the belief M-sensitive.

Now we'll be able to say that the grandmother's belief that her grandson is well obtains the status of knowledge from the evidence

---

[23]   R. Nozick 1981: 179.

that she gathers during his visit provided that she doesn't believe he is well in the nearest world in which he is unwell and she arrives at her belief whether or not he is well by the same method.

But not all cases of evidential knowledge can be handled so easily. The reason why the model is suitable for this case is that the sensory evidence gathered by the grandmother can be described as resulting from the application of a method (call it casual inspection) capable of producing the belief that her grandson is not well as well as the belief that he is well. This enables us to single out the worlds in which she would have to refrain from believing that her grandson is well in order for her actual belief to be M-sensitive – the nearest worlds in which he is not well and she arrives at her belief whether or not he is well by casual inspection.

In other cases in which q provides adequate evidence for p, belief in p cannot be described as resulting from the application of a method for arriving at a belief whether or not p that could also be used if p were false. Consider cases in which q is the positive result of a test with no false positives but lots of false negatives. The worlds that we would need to look at to determine the M-sensitivity of S's belief that p would be the nearest non-p worlds in which S arrives at a belief whether or not p on the basis of that method. But not-p worlds can be expected to be not-q worlds, and in light of the evidential irrelevance of not-q to whether or not p, it is not clear under what circumstances we should say of a not-q world that in this world S has arrived at her belief whether or not p on the basis of the method that she used in actuality for forming her belief that p. Presumably it would have to be a world in which the evidential irrelevance of not-q for the truth value of p is not outweighed by any proposition that S believes and considers evidentially relevant for the truth value of p – i.e. a world in which S regards all the propositions that she believes, including not-q, as evidentially irrelevant to whether or not p. But then describing S's suspension of judgment on p as resulting specifically from the q-method would seem entirely arbitrary.

The case for describing S's counterfactual suspension of judgment on p as resulting from the same method that she actually employed for forming her belief that p is particularly weak in cases in which the serendipitous nature of the evidence that actually lead to belief in p would make it unlikely that, if the evidence didn't obtain, its failure to obtain would even occur to S. Suppose that Mary's son disappeared years ago. One day she finds on the street a copy of today's newspaper with what she conclusively identifies as her son's signature written on it. It is natural to suppose that this discovery can bestow on her belief that her son is alive the status of knowledge. But accounting for this knowledge in terms of ES* would require considering situations in which Mary refrains from believing that her son is alive as a result of her realisation that she hasn't found on the street a copy of today's newspaper with her son's signature on it. And it is hard to see how this realisation could ever be the main factor in Mary's counterfactual decision not to believe that her son is alive.

The general point that these observations illustrate is that the way in which evidence can confer on S's true belief that p the status of knowledge can't always be naturally characterised in terms of the application of a method for arriving at a belief as to whether or not p. But describing evidence in these terms is unavoidable as soon as we decide to characterise the way in which evidence can confer on a belief the status of knowledge in terms of the sensitivity of the belief.

My proposal is, then, that the risk of error regarding S's true belief that p can be brought under control either by the protection that results from belief sensitivity or by the assurance that error is not present afforded by evidence. In normal circumstances, both forms of control go together. On the one hand, if the facts about the subject's cognitive devices that make her belief sensitive are known to her, they will provide her with adequate evidence of its truth. On the other hand, when S's belief that p is based on adequate evidence, normally it will also be sensitive: if p were false, the evidence wouldn't obtain, the subject wouldn't believe in the evidence, and the subject wouldn't believe that p. Nevertheless, either form of control can in principle be present in the absence of the other. We have just seen how evidence without sensitivity can arise. Sensitive belief in the absence of evidence is also a possibility, so long as our notion of evidence incorporates even a minimal accessibility constraint. Cases of this kind are provided by beliefs whose sensitivity results from reliable sub-personal belief-forming devices of which the subject cannot be aware without sophisticated scientific research.[24] What I am proposing is that either form of risk control will suffice on its own to satisfy the ROE constraint.

---

[24] Notice that a constraint that requires evidence whenever there is a substantial risk of error will be too strong if sensitive belief is regarded as an adequate form of risk control. My principle EW (see my "Externalism, Skepticism and the Problem of Easy Knowledge") would have to be modified accordingly.

José L. Zalabardo

5. Risk, Knowledge and Scepticism

We can now use the ideas I have presented to provide a formulation of the ROE constraint:[25]

ROE: If S believes that p and p is true, then S knows that p only if either p is true throughout the relevant sphere or S's belief that p is sensitive or S has identified adequate evidence for p.[26]

Notice that the ROE constraint is only a necessary condition for knowledge. It's certainly not universally sufficient. All beliefs in necessary truths satisfy the ROE constraint trivially. A similar point applies to belief in true natural laws.[27] Knowledge in these cases might require evidence or sensitivity even if the ROE constraint doesn't call for it. Nevertheless, I want to put forward the hypothesis that these are the only cases in which the situation might arise. In all other cases, knowledge requires evidence or sensitivity only if the ROE constraint calls for it. I am going to refer to this hypothesis as the *Limitation Clause* (LC).

I want to turn now to considering how ROE (and LC) can be used for dealing with the standard lines of reasoning in support of premise 1 of the canonical argument – the claim that we don't know that sceptical hypotheses don't obtain. The claim has been defended by two different routes, corresponding to the two forms of control of the risk of error contemplated by the ROE constraint.[28] Some have argued, on the one hand, that the reason why I don't know not-BIV is that I don't have adequate evidence in support of this proposition. Furthermore, this predicament can't be overcome, since the BIV hypothesis is precisely designed so that no evidence that I might conceivably gather could support its

---

[25]   The set of beliefs that satisfy the ROE constraint for a person at a time can be inductively defined. The base will contain those true beliefs of the subject which are either sensitive or true throughout the Relevant Sphere. And the inductive clause will stipulate that if the set contains S's belief that q and S's belief that q is sensitive to p, then it also contains S's belief that p.

[26]   There are important connections between the ROE constraint and the notion of safety used in some recent accounts of knowledge. See E. Sosa 1999, D. Pritchard 2005. See also Tim Williamson's notion of *safety from error*: T. Williamson 2000: 123–31.

[27]   Thanks to Ciara Fairley for helping me see this.

[28]   For a discussion of the relative merits of these strategies, see A. Brueckner 1994: 828–30.

negation.[29] Others have argued, on the other hand, that I don't know not-BIV because my belief in this proposition is insensitive – if it were false, if I were in fact a brain in a vat, I would still believe that I'm not.[30]

I think that the basic premise of each of these arguments has to be conceded to the sceptic. My belief in not-BIV is certainly not sensitive. And I can't obtain adequate evidence in its support.[31] It follows that the risk of error of my belief in not-BIV is not controlled either by sensitivity or by evidence. However, armed with the ROE constraint (and LC), we can object to the transition from each of these premises to the conclusion that we don't know not-BIV. The reason is obvious. From the fact that my belief in not-BIV is insensitive, and its risk of error is not evidentially controlled, it follows that the risk of error is not under control.[32] But lack of control is a problem only when the risk is substantial. And in the case of sceptical hypotheses, the risk is not substantial – the Relevant Sphere contains no worlds in which they are true. This means that my beliefs to the effect that they don't obtain satisfy the ROE constraint even though their risk of error is not under control. They satisfy the ROE constraint by virtue of the sheer remoteness of the worlds in which they are false. As far as the ROE constraint goes, I know not-BIV even though my belief is insensitive and its risk of error is not evidentially controlled. I know this 'by default' – because things would have to be radically different from the way they are in order for my belief to be false.

---

[29] This is the strategy for supporting premise 1 of the canonical argument endorsed by Dretske. See F. Dretske 1970: 1016.

[30] This is the strategy adopted by Nozick (see R. Nozick 1981: 200–3). Notice that, as Brueckner has pointed out, someone who, unlike Nozick, endorses the canonical argument, would be ill-advised to defend its first premise in this way, as the claim that knowledge requires sensitivity would undermine the Closure principle, which is the main source of support for the second premise of the argument (see A. Brueckner 1994: 828).

[31] This point has been contested. See J. Pryor, "The skeptic and the Dogmatist". Arguing that I cannot obtain evidence for the conclusion that sceptical hypotheses don't obtain would require imposing additional conditions on the possession of adequate evidence. I have discussed this issue in "Wright on Moore".

[32] Notice that neither argument on its own would suffice to establish this. Both lack of evidential control and insensitivity would have to be invoked in order to obtain the conclusion.

Of course we might be wrong about this. Worlds in which the sceptical hypotheses are true might be much closer that we think they are, and the Relevant Sphere might contain some of them. And, needless to say, the actual world might be such a world. If the sceptic could provide adequate support for these claims, we would have to accept her conclusion. But the sceptic won't expect to have much success through this route. Her hope was to show that, even if things were as we believe them to be, and even if they had to be as different as we think they would have to be in order for sceptical hypotheses to be true, our beliefs would still not have the status of knowledge. The sceptic's argumentative repertoire contains no resources for establishing that sceptical hypotheses are true either in the actual world or in nearby worlds.

In conclusion, according to the ROE constraint (and LC), it follows from the remoteness of worlds in which sceptical hypotheses are true that I need neither evidence nor sensitivity in order to know that they don't obtain. The remoteness of these worlds is an empirical hypothesis which might turn out to be false, but the sceptic has no argument against it. Therefore, it follows from the ROE constraint (and LC) that the sceptic has no cogent argument for the conclusion that I don't know that sceptical hypotheses don't obtain. I believe I do, and the sceptic's arguments give me no reason to abandon my belief.

6. Pryor's Dogmatism

DeRose uses the label *Moorean* for positions that seek to resist the canonical argument by rejecting its first premise.[33] I have argued that there is a Moorean core in DeRose's contextualist response to the canonical argument. Then I have put forward an invariantist version of the Moorean response. There are other positions in the recent literature that also answer to this description. One that enjoys special prominence is Jim Pryor's dogmatism.[34] In this section I'd like to spell out briefly how the view that I am putting forward is related to Pryor's.

There is one fundamental point on which my position agrees with Pryor's. As fellow Mooreans, we both think that we can resist the sceptic's contention that we don't know that sceptical hypotheses don't obtain. The point at which our views come apart is in our

---

[33]   See K. DeRose 1995: 41.

[34]   See J. Pryor 2000. For another proposal along these lines, see T. Black 2002.

explanations of how this knowledge is possible. One way of bringing out the difference is to consider an argument for the conclusion that I don't know not-BIV which plays an important role in Pryor's discussion, even though he doesn't formulate it in exactly these terms:

A. You can't have knowledge of not-BIV that doesn't rest in part on things that you know by perception.[35]

B. You can't have knowledge of not-BIV that rests in part on things that you know by perception.

Therefore:

C. You can't know not-BIV.[36]

Pryor's strategy for resisting the conclusion of this argument consists in rejecting B. He argues that we know certain things by perception prior to knowing not-BIV, and that knowledge of not-BIV can then rest on these things that we know by perception. In this way, Pryor can satisfy the constraint on knowledge of not-BIV imposed by A, which he finds very plausible.[37]

It seems to me that intuition is firmly against the thought that knowledge of not-BIV can rest on things that you know by perception – e.g. that you have hands or that it's raining. Hence, in my view, the fact that a position explains knowledge of not-BIV in these terms, as Pryor's does, should count, other things being equal, as a reason for rejecting the position. In any case, this is not the place to assess Pryor's rejection of B.[38] My goal is to explain how his strategy differs from mine. And the difference is that, on my position, the way to deal with the argument under discussion is to reject premise A. According to this strategy, the contention expressed by premise B – that my knowledge of not-BIV cannot rest on things that I know by perception – doesn't threaten my knowledge of not-BIV. For this knowledge doesn't have to rest on other knowledge. It results, as far as the ROE constraint goes, from the fact that there are no BIV worlds in the Relevant Sphere.[39] Hence the position that I'm advocating enables us to subscribe premise B, and I regard this, as stated above, as a distinct advantage of this position over Pryor's.

---

[35] A claim of this form (substituting the evil-demon hypothesis) is equivalent to premise (5) in Pryor's article (2000: 524).

[36] Cf. claim (8) in Pryor's article (Ibid. 528).

[37] Cf. Ibid., 529.

[38] I address this question in Zalabardo *forthcoming*.

[39] I think this view is different from each of the positions opposed to A (Pryor's premise (5)) that Pryor considers (cf. J. Pryor 2000: 524).

José L. Zalabardo

7. A Revised Proposal

I think that the account presented in previous sections provides a good match for our intuitions concerning propositions that are false in fairly close possible worlds (e.g. I have a broken fingernail) and for propositions that are false only in very remote possible worlds (e.g. I am not a brain in a vat). And these are the kinds of proposition that figure in the canonical argument. However the nearest possible world in which a proposition is false can be at any distance from the actual world between these two extremes. And for propositions for which this distance falls towards the middle of these two extremes, the results are less satisfactory.

Let me refer to the distance between the actual world and the nearest world in which p is false as *p's falsehood distance*. According to our formulation of the ROE constraint, the level of risk control required for your belief that p to have the status of knowledge is a function of p's falsehood distance – but the function only yields two values: zero for falsehood distances greater than the radius of the relevant sphere, and maximum for all the rest. This means that significant differences between the falsehood distances of propositions (e.g. a minimal falsehood distance vs. one only marginally smaller than the radius of the relevant sphere) will have no effect on what level of risk control is required for knowledge. And very small differences (e.g. between falsehood distances marginally smaller and marginally greater than the radius of the relevant sphere) will have a huge effect – the difference between needing full control and needing no control at all.

These anomalies are brought to the fore by some cases that are discussed in the literature on the canonical argument. Consider, e.g. the scenario presented by Dretske in his argument against Closure, in which someone, call her Naari, comes to believe that the animals in a zoo enclosure are zebras by looking at them.[40] Intuitively we might want to say that this belief has the status of knowledge. However, the following argument would seem to rule out this claim:

Naari doesn't know that the animals in the zebra enclosure are not mules cleverly disguised by the zoo authorities in order to look like zebras.

If Naari doesn't know that the animals in the zebra enclosure are not mules cleverly disguised by the zoo authorities in order to look like zebras, then she doesn't know that they are zebras.

[40]   See F. Dretske 1970.

84

How I Know I'm Not a Brain in a Vat

Therefore:

Naari doesn't know that the animals in the zebra enclosure are zebras.

If we wanted to apply to this argument the strategy that I have presented for the canonical argument, we would need to maintain that Naari's belief that the animals are not cleverly disguised mules satisfies the ROE constraint. But this doesn't seem very plausible. Notice, first, that if we said that the falsehood distance of the proposition that the animals are not cleverly disguised mules ($\sim$M) is greater than the radius of the Relevant Sphere, it would follow that Naari's belief in $\sim$M would satisfy the ROE constraint even if its risk of error were completely uncontrolled. And this doesn't seem right. Intuition dictates, or so I will assume, that knowledge requires some control in this case. From this we seem forced to conclude that the falsehood distance of $\sim$M is less than the radius of the relevant sphere. But this means that the ROE constraint will require as much risk control in this case as in any other, and the level of risk control present in this case would be clearly insufficient in other cases. Naari's belief is clearly not sensitive, and she wouldn't normally have adequate evidence either. She has some evidence of a vague sort (e.g. zoo authorities don't tend to do that sort of thing), but it clearly doesn't meet the standards of the notion of evidence that I have presented.

I find this outcome counterintuitive. The falsehood distance of $\sim$M is intermediate between the falsehood distances of $\sim$BIV, on the one hand, and of the proposition that I have a broken fingernail, or that the animals in the enclosure are zebras, on the other. The difference between how things are and how they would have to be in order for the enclosure to contain convincingly disguised mules is much greater than the difference between how things are and how they would have to be in order for the enclosure not to contain zebras, but much smaller than the difference between the way things are and the way they would have to be in order for me to be a brain in a vat. I think this fact should be reflected in what level of control of the risk of error would be required in order for Naari's belief in $\sim$M to satisfy the ROE constraint: some control should be required but not as much as with propositions with much smaller falsehood distances. In general, the level of risk control required should vary gradually with the falsehood distance of the proposition in question. In the remainder I want to put forward a revised formulation of the ROE constraint that satisfies this desideratum.

85

José L. Zalabardo

The revised proposal will make use of propositions to which I shall refer as *probabilistic counterfactuals* – counterfactuals with a probabilistic conclusion, e.g. *if Tony Blair hadn't won the last election, fox hunting would probably still be legal*. These counterfactuals sustain comparisons of probability. We can say, e.g. *if Tony Blair hadn't won the last election, fox hunting would be more likely to be legal than smoking cannabis would be*. Idealising from these comparisons, we can assign for all facts A and B a numerical value between 0 and 1 to the probability that A wouldn't obtain if B didn't obtain, represented as $CProb(\sim A/\sim B)$.[41] We can refer to this value as A's *sensitivity* to B, and say that A is *k-sensitive* to B when $CProb(\sim A/\sim B) = \text{k}$. This notion enables us to specify a continuously variable degree of control of the risk of error as a necessary condition for knowledge. The risk of error of S's belief that p will be controlled to a degree k between 0 and 1 just in case either S's belief that p is k-sensitive (to p) or S has identified k-sensitive evidence for p.

To complete the model, we just need to determine what degree of control will be required for a given belief that p to satisfy the ROE constraint. My proposal is that this will be determined by the falsehood distance of p. Thus we postulate the *control-requirement* function, *cr*, pairing each true proposition p with the number between 0 and 1 that represents the level of control of the risk of error that would be required in order for a belief that p to satisfy the ROE constraint. In order to play this role, the control-requirement function will have to satisfy a few basic conditions. First, it will have to assign the same value to propositions with the same falsehood distance. Second, if the falsehood distance of p is greater than the falsehood distance of q, then p won't receive a greater value than q. Finally, we can add a condition that calibrates the function to the Relevant Sphere: a proposition will have to receive a non-zero value if and only if its falsehood distance is smaller than the radius of the Relevant Sphere.

Using the control-requirement function, we can now provide our new formulation of the ROE constraint:

ROE* If S believes that p and p is true, then S knows that p only if either S's belief that p is cr(p)-sensitive (to p) or S has identified cr(p)-sensitive evidence for p.

Let me close by considering briefly how this account would enable us to deal with Naari's belief that the animals in the enclosure are not

---

[41]   Nozick uses these counterfactuals in his account of evidence based on probability. See R. Nozick 1981: 251–63.

cleverly disguised mules. In light of our previous discussion of the case, we should expect cr to assign a low but non-zero value to the proposition that the animals are not cleverly disguised mules. This means that the ROE constraint will require a certain level of risk control in this case, but not as much as in other cases, e.g. her belief that the animals are zebras or my belief that I have a broken fingernail. Hence it is possible in principle that the weak evidence that she has for $\sim$M provides her belief with a sufficient level of risk control. This would be so if the probability that her evidence didn't obtain if the animals were cleverly disguised mules is higher than the (low) value that cr assigns to this proposition. Hence, while yielding the same results as our previous proposal for propositions with very large or very small falsehood distances, the present account appears to have the resources to provide a more satisfactory treatment of the intermediate cases.

University College London

References

Black, Tim. (2002) "A Moorean Response to Brain-In-A-Vat Scepticism." *Australasian Journal of Philosophy* **80**, 148–63.

Brueckner, Anthony. (1994) "The Structure of the Skeptical Argument." *Philosophy and Phenomenological Research* **54**, 827–35.

DeRose, Keith. (1995) "Solving the Skeptical Problem." *Philosophical Review* **104**, 1–52.

———— (1999) "Contextualism: An Explanation and Defense." In *The Blackwell Guide to Epistemology*, (eds.) Ernest Sosa and John Greco, 187–205. Malden, Massachusetts and Oxford: Blackwell.

———— (2004) "Sosa, Safety, Sensitivity, and Skeptical Hypotheses." In *Ernest Sosa and His Critics*, (ed.) John Greco, 22–41. Malden, Massachusetts and Oxford: Blackwell.

Descartes, René. (1984) "Meditations on First Philosophy." In *The Philosophical Writings of Descartes. Volume II*, (eds.) John Cottingham, Robert Stoothoff and Dugald Murdoch, 1–62. Cambridge: Cambridge University Press.

Dretske, Fred. (1970) "Epistemic Operators." *Journal of Philosophy* **67**, 1007–23.

Nozick, Robert. (1981) *Philosophical Explanations*. Cambridge, Massachusetts: Harvard University Press.

Pritchard, Duncan. (2005) *Epistemic Luck*. Oxford: Clarendon.

Pryor, James. (2000) "The Skeptic and the Dogmatist." *Noûs* **34**, 517–49.

Putnam, Hilary. (1981) *Reason, Truth and History*. Cambridge: Cambridge University Press.

Sosa, Ernest. (1999) "How to Defeat Opposition to Moore." In *Philosophical Perspectives*, **13**, *Epistemology*, (ed.) James E. Tomberlin, 141–53. Malden, Massachusetts and Oxford: Blackwell.

Williamson, Tim. (2000) *Knowledge and Its Limits*. Oxford: Oxford University Press.

Zalabardo, José L. (2005) "Externalism, Skepticism and the Problem of Easy Knowledge." *Philosophical Review* **114**, 33–61.

———— (*forthcoming*) "Wright on Moore." In *Wittgenstein, Epistemology and Mind. Themes from the Philosophy of Crispin Wright*, (ed.) Annalisa Coliva. Oxford: Oxford University Press.

Belief, Reason & Logic*

SCOTT STURGEON

I aim to do four things in this paper: sketch a conception of belief, apply epistemic norms to it in an orthodox way, canvass a need for more norms than found in orthodoxy, and then check the relation between orthodox and new norms by looking at logic's role within epistemic theory. A perspective will unfold on which the epistemology of "coarse" belief – also known as "full" or "binary" belief – springs from the epistemology of "fine" belief – also known as confidence. But the epistemology of fine belief will be shown to outstrip the epistemology of point-valued subjective probability. Clarifying the overall picture will lead to a critical discussion of a view recently defended by David Christensen.

1. Belief

It is obvious that we believe, disbelieve and suspend judgement in things. This is a manifest fact. It is obvious that we invest levels of confidence in things. This too is a manifest fact. These sides of our mind turn on "coarse" and "fine" belief respectively. The former involves a notion of belief slotting into a three-fold scheme of psychological categorization. The latter involves a notion of belief slotting into an indefinitely large scheme of psychological categorization.

Although it is obvious that we enjoy coarse and fine belief, it is not obvious how they relate to one another. What interesting metaphysical relation exists, if any, between coarse and fine belief? And how do their epistemologies fit together, if at all? We shall assume a Lockean take on these issues. Specifically: we shall assume that coarse belief is ontologically nothing over and above sufficiently strong confidence, that disbelief is ontologically nothing over and above sufficiently weak confidence, and that suspended judgement is ontologically nothing over and above confidence middling in strength – confidence

*   This paper is based on a talk given to the Royal Institute of Philosophy in 2006. I thank the Royal Institute for its invitation to speak, the Royal Audience for its useful feedback, David Christensen for sound advice on §4, Dorothy Edgington and Mark Kaplan for years of supervision, and Maja Spener for help with every aspect of the paper.

doi:10.1017/S1358246109000058   © The Royal Institute of Philosophy and the contributors 2009

neither strong enough for coarse belief nor weak enough for disbelief. Our launch point will be this picture:

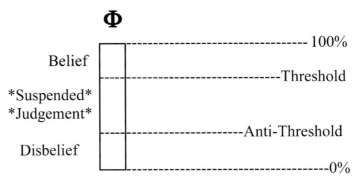

As confidence in Φ goes up and down, one's status as a believer, disbeliever or suspender of judgement is there by fixed. To believe coarsely − on this Lockean picture − is to have sufficiently strong confidence, to *dis*believe coarsely is to have sufficiently weak confidence, and to suspend judgement is to have confidence neither sufficiently strong for coarse belief nor sufficiently weak for coarse disbelief.[1]

Our guiding slogan will be "Confidence first!" Confidence will be taken as explanatorily basic; and the explanatory import of coarse belief, if any − together with the explanatory import of coarse epistemology, if any − will be shown to derive fully from the explanatory import of confidence and its epistemology. It will also be shown that the explanatory import of coarse belief and its epistemology are theoretically fundamental. A key burden of the paper is to explain how these claims can all be true.

2. Reason

We turn to the orthodox application of epistemic norms to levels of confidence. That application involves thinking of ideally rational

---

[1]   We shall also assume that "sufficiency" is a vague and contextually-variable matter. The stars surrounding suspended judgement in the diagram mark the fact that I do not accept this bit of the Lockean picture. By my lights suspended judgement is a *sui generis* kind of attitude, a primitive kind of 'committed neutrality' (as Selim Berker suggested I call it). Arguing that point would take us beyond the scope of this paper. For more on the nature of coarse belief, disbelief and suspended judgement, as well as the belief-making threshold, see Sturgeon *forthcominga* and *forthcomingb*: ch. 6.

levels of confidence as point-valued subjective probabilities – or "credences" as they are known. The mathematics of the model need not concern us. Two simple rules – endorsed by the approach – serve nicely to ground our discussion.

The first is the two-cell partition principle for credence:

If Φ_1 and Φ_2 form into a logical partition, and your rational point-valued subjective probability for them is cr_1 & cr_2 respectively, then:
$(cr_1 + cr_2) = 100\%$.

The idea here is both simple and compelling. If two claims form into a logical partition – if logic guarantees exactly one of them is true – and your credence in them is cr_1 & cr_2 respectively, then to be ideally rational those credences should sum to 100%. Ideally rational credence in Φ and $\neg\Phi$, for instance, adds up in that way – it sums to unity – and so it should be with any two claims which make for a logical partition.

The second rule of thought endorsed by the orthodox application of norms to levels of confidence is the logical implication principle for credence:

If Φ_1 logically implies Φ_2, and your rational credence in Φ_1 is cr_1, then you should not invest credence in Φ_2 less than cr_1.

The idea here is also simple and compelling: in the epistemic ideal one never invests less confidence in one thing than one invests in something from which it follows. When you are rationally 70% sure of Φ, for instance, you should never be 65% sure of **($\Phi v \Psi$)**.

By adding more rules like these a position is created known as *Probabilism*. It is a view on which ideally rational degrees of belief are measured by point-valued probability functions, and ideally rational degrees of belief rationally change by conditionalisation (or perhaps Richard Jeffrey's generalisation of that rule). If such a picture is right, however, point-valued probability is central to ideal rationality. Point-valued probability is the metaphysical and explanatory linchpin in the area, the theoretical un-moved mover, the key to fine belief and its rational idealisation.

So what of coarse belief and its epistemology?

Well, Probabilism and Locke's take on coarse belief jointly entail that the metaphysics of coarse belief fully derives from point-valued subjective probability. In turn that suggests that the epistemology of coarse belief is itself fully derivative; and this leads to a perspective common to Bayesian epistemology: namely, the view that the epistemology of coarse belief is unimportant, the view that the epistemology of coarse belief is at best a by-product of Probabilism.

Here is Richard Jeffrey vocalising the sentiment:

> By 'belief' I mean the thing that goes along with valuation in decision-making: degree-of-belief, or subjective probability, or personal probability, or grade of credence. I do not care what you call it because I can tell you what it is, and how to measure it, within limits...Nor am I disturbed by the fact that our ordinary notion of belief is only vestigially present in the notion of degree of belief. I am inclined to think Ramsey sucked the marrow out of the ordinary notion, and used it to nourish a more adequate view.[2]

And here is Robert Stalnaker crystallising the thought to be resisted:

> One could easily enough define a concept of belief which identified it with high subjective or epistemic probability (probability greater than some specified number between one-half and one), but it is not clear what the point of doing so would be. Once a subjective or epistemic probability value is assigned to a proposition, there is nothing more to be said about its epistemic status. Probabilist decision theory gives a complete account of how probability values, including high ones, ought to guide behaviour, in both the context of inquiry and the application of belief outside of this context. So what could be the point of selecting an interval near the top of the probability scale and conferring on the propositions whose probability falls in that interval the honorific title 'believed'?[3]

The worry behind each of these quotes is obvious: *if* coarse epistemology springs from its fine cousin via a belief-making threshold – if it is Lockean, in our terms – then coarse epistemology is pointless; it is at best a theoretical shadow cast by real explanatory theory (Probabilism); and it is at worst an un-refined bit everyday lore to be jettisoned like other bits of quotidian nonsense.

3. More Norms Please

My view is that the perspective just sketched is mistaken. In turn I think that because two other things seem true: Probabilism seems

[2] Jeffrey 1970: 132.
[3] Stalnaker 1984: 148.

to be an incomplete epistemology of confidence; and the complete epistemology of confidence seems to contain coarse belief as such. To see this, consider a few thought experiments.

Case 1

When faced with a black box you are rationally certain of this much: the box is filled with a huge number of balls; they have been thoroughly mixed; exactly 85% of them are red; touching one will not change its colour. You reach into the box, grab a ball, and wonder about its colour. You have no view about anything else relevant to your question. How confident should you be that you hold a red ball?

You should be 85% confident, of course. Your confidence in the claim that you hold a red ball is well modelled by a position in Probabilism's "attitude space":

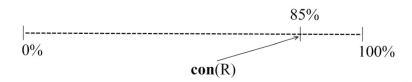

Here we have one attitude *ruled in* by evidence and others *ruled out*. The case suggests a principle I aim to defend:

Out-by-In   Attitudes get ruled out by evidence because others get ruled in.

In Case 1, after all, it seems intuitively right that everything but 70% credence is ruled out by your evidence precisely because that very credence is itself ruled in.

Case 2

Now the set up is just as before save this time you know that exactly 80-to-90% of balls in the box are red. How confident should you be that you hold a red ball?

You should be exactly 80-to-90% confident, of course. Your confidence in the claim that you hold a red ball *cannot* be well modelled with a position in Probabilism's attitude space. Your evidence is too rough for that. Certain attitudes within Probabilism's attitude space – within credal space, as we might put it – are ruled out by your evidence in Case 2. But no attitude in credal space is itself ruled in. This puts pressure on the Out-by-In principle.

I want to resist that pressure by insisting that there are more attitudes in our psychology than are dreamt of in Probabilist epistemology. There are more kinds of confidence than credence. Moreover, non-credal confidence is often the right epistemic reaction to everyday evidence. Each of these points is important, if true, so consider them in turn.

A moment's reflection suggests that there are more kinds of confidence than credence. After all, propositional attitudes are individuated functionally. Point-valued subjective probabilities are highly specific functional properties. Being 37% sure that Φ, for instance, is a highly-specific functional property indexed to Φ's truth. There are good questions about its metaphysics and epistemology, to be sure – does it get pinned down by theory? does our knowledge of it come through knowledge of betting behaviour? And so on. But questions like these are not our concern. Our focus is solely on the fact that point-valued subjective probabilities – like being 37% sure that Φ – are highly specific functional properties. Their functional nature is guaranteed by functionalism about propositional attitudes. Their high specificity is guaranteed by their strength being measured by *point-valued* probability functions.

Such functional properties are not the only explanatorily-basic functional properties in our psychology. It is perfectly possible to be more coarsely organised. When a pure Probabilist agent takes an attitudinal stand on Φ – when she invests credence in Φ – she does so by manifesting a highly-specific functional property, one whose nature is indexed to Φ's truth and whose relative strength is measured – under idealisation, at least – with point-valued probability. We needn't do anything like that. It is possible that we manifest coarser functions in our basic psychology, coarser functions indexed to Φ in exactly the way that credence lent to Φ is so indexed. But that means we can adopt a propositional attitude outside the psychological repertoire of a pure Probabilist agent. We can adopt a non-credal level of confidence. We can adopt what I call a *thick confidence*.

To get a feel for this, think back to Case 2. Evidence in it demands more than a point in credal space. It demands something more like a region instead. Evidence in Case 2 rules in a thick confidence like this:

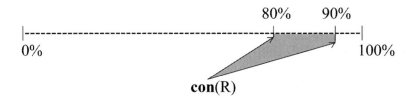

con(R)

Everyday evidence tends not to rule in credence, being too coarse-grained for that job. This does not mean that everyday evidence tends not to rule in confidence. It just means that such evidence tends to warrant thick confidence.[4]

The point to be emphasised is of first importance to epistemic theory: *evidence and attitude should match in character*. Precision in evidence should prompt precision in attitude. Imprecision in evidence should prompt imprecision in attitude. Evidence is normally imprecise – in everyday life, anyway – and so thick confidence is normally the right attitudinal reaction to it. Yet thick confidence is something over and above credence. It is functionally too coarse to be any kind of credence.

This opens up notional space, at least, for a *reduction* of Lockean coarse belief to confidence; and in turn that softens the conceptual ground for a confidence-theoretic understanding of basic norms for coarse belief. After all, suppose coarse belief is Lockean. Then coarse belief will be identical to a certain thick confidence. Specifically, it will be identical to thick confidence stretching from the belief-making threshold to certainty. The picture will be this:

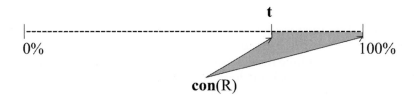

con(R)

---

4   In fact the sharp-edged nature of evidence in Case 2 is itself uncommon. A much more typical example would involve knowing merely that there were *roughly* 80–90% red balls in the box, or that *most* of the balls are red. This introduces the fact that imprecision in evidence can aptly warrant a *vague* propositional attitude. But the issues surrounding this fact are best left aside in this paper. Further discussion can be found in Sturgeon *forthcominga* and *forthcomingb*: ch. 6.

Probabilism may give a complete account of rational credence. It does not give a complete account of rational confidence. The view entails that ideally rational agents always assign, in reaction to their evidence, point-valued subjective probability to questions of interest. It is obvious that this is not so. *Often* our evidence is too coarse for subjective probability. *Normally* our evidence is too coarse for that tool; and when that is so epistemic perfection rules out credence in favour of thick confidence. There should be character match between attitude and evidence on which it is based.

We deal in coarse evidence most of the time. As a result, we should mostly adopt an attitude at the heart of both coarse and fine epistemology. We should mostly adopt a thick confidence. Often that confidence will spread from the belief-making threshold to certainty; and when it does everyday evidence will warrant nothing finer-grained than coarse belief. Coarse epistemology can be of theoretical moment even if Probabilism is the full story of rational credence, for coarse epistemology captures a central concern of everyday rationality.

4. Logic and epistemic theory

We have before us a picture of fine-grained epistemology. I close by elaborating that picture in three steps: first I pose a question about logic's role within epistemic theory; then I sketch David Christensen's answer to that question; then I pose a worry for his answer. The result will help clarify how basic norms for thick confidence – and hence basic norms for coarse belief – are best conceived.

Question: what is logic's fundamental role in epistemic theory?

Probabilism invites the view that logic's role in that theory is echoed directly by its basic role in shaping point-valued probability functions. The idea is that logic helps shape rational belief – in the first instance, anyway – in just the way it shapes point-valued probability functions. Once thick confidence enters the scene, however, it is unclear what to say about logic and rational belief. After all, thick confidence is not usefully modelled by a single point-valued probability function. This suggests the injection of thick confidence into epistemic theory prompts a non-trivial shift in view about logic's basic role within epistemology. It suggests the epistemology of thick confidence should re-conceive logic's role in shaping rational belief.

David Christensen rejects that idea, defending instead a Probabilist answer to our question about logic even after thick confidence – or 'spread out credence', as he calls it – is found within epistemic theory. Christensen notes that thick confidence is naturally modelled by richly-membered sets of point-valued probability functions. He infers from this that an epistemology of thick confidence will preserve Probabilism's take on logic sketched in the last paragraph. "On any such view," he says

> ideally rational degrees of belief are constrained by the logical structure of the propositions believed, and the constraints are based on the principles of probability. Wherever an agent does have precise degrees of belief, those degrees are constrained by probabilistic coherence in the standard way. Where her credences are spread out, they are still constrained by coherence, albeit in a more subtle way. Thus the normative claim that rationality allows, or even requires, spread-out credences does not undermine the basic position that I have been defending [in this book]: that logic constrains ideal rationality by means of probabilistic conditions on degrees of confidence.[5]

This passage trades – rather tacitly – on a subtle-but-mistaken projection. Specifically, it trades on a mistaken projection of this

(a)   The way large-scale features of a model of thick confidence are metaphysically grounded

onto

(b)   The way large-scale features of thick confidence are metaphysically grounded.

Let me explain.

Suppose we model ideally rational thick confidence with sets of point-valued probability functions.[6] In the event, large-scale properties of the model will be reductively explained by the workings of (collections of) point-valued probability functions; for entities used in the model are literally built from such functions. Further still – and for the same reason – dynamical properties the model will be defined directly by the workings of point-valued probability functions. The basic explanation of our model's large-scale properties, then, will come reductively from the workings of such functions. In turn that means the fundamental role of

---

[5]   Christensen 2004: 150.

[6]   A typical approach would use convex sets of point-valued probability functions to model thick confidence. It would also apply conditionalisation (where defined) to members of those sets to model rational shift in thick confidence. See Joyce 2005 for a nice discussion of the approach's strengths.

logic – in determining the large-scale features of our model – will itself come reductively from logic's role in shaping point-valued probability functions.

But that does not mean that the fundamental role of logic in shaping *the phenomena being modelled* – thick confidence – itself derives from logic's role in shaping the phenomena modelled by point-valued probability functions. We must sharply distinguish the metaphysics of entities which model thick confidence from the metaphysics of thick confidence itself. On the approach under discussion, entities used to model thick confidence are built exclusively from point-valued probability functions. The nature of those entities derives exclusively from the nature of functions out of which they are built. But thick confidence is not built from credence; and its nature does not derive from the nature of credence.[7] The metaphysics of our model misleads about the metaphysics of the phenomena being modelled; for the metaphysics of sets of point-valued probability functions fails to echo the metaphysics of thick confidence. The former is reductively shaped by probabilistic atoms (point-valued probability functions). The latter is not reductively shaped by anything. It is non-reductive through and through. Thick confidence is an explanatorily basic bit of our psychology.

To see this more clearly, recall the two-cell partition principle for credence:

> If Φ_1 and Φ_2 form into a logical partition, and your rational point-valued subjective probability for them is cr_1 & cr_2 respectively, then:
> $(cr_1 + cr_2) = 100\%$.

A generalisation of this thought applies to thick confidence. It can be sketched by appeal to intervals in the unit interval rather than points in that interval. The result is a two-cell partition principle for confidence:

> If Φ_1 and Φ_2 form into a logical partition, and your rational confidence in them is $[a,b]$ & $[c,d]$ respectively, then: $(a + d) = 100\%$ and $(b + c) = 100\%$.

If you are 20-to-30% confident in Φ, for instance, you should be 70-to-80% confident in $\neg\Phi$. And so on. But notice: the two-celled partition principle for credence is a limit case of the two-celled partition principle for confidence. The latter does not hold because the

---

[7] Indeed thick confidence cannot be built from credence. The functional nature of attitudes makes that impossible.

former holds, not even because the former holds in a range of cases. The order of explanation goes from general fact to limit-case instance. The two-cell partition principle for credence holds *as* a limit case of the two-cell partition principle for confidence.

Or recall the logical implication principle for credence:

If Φ_1 logically implies Φ_2, and your rational credence in Φ_1 is cr_1, then you should not invest credence in Φ_2 less than cr_1.

A generalisation of this thought applies to thick confidence. And it too can be sketched by appeal to intervals in the unit interval rather than points in that interval. The result is a logical implication principle for confidence:

If Φ_1 logically implies Φ_2, and your rational confidence in Φ_1 is $[a, b]$, then you should not invest confidence $[c, d]$ in Φ_2 when c is less than a.

When you are 70-to-80% sure of Φ, for instance, you should not invest a confidence $[c, d]$ in $(\Phi v \Psi)$ when c is less than 70%. But notice: the logical implication principle for credence is a limit case of the logical implication principle for confidence. The latter does not hold because the former holds, not even because the former holds in a range of cases. The order of explanation goes from general fact to limit-case instance. The two-cell partition principle for credence holds *as* a limit case of the two-cell partition principle for confidence.

Thick confidence is normally modelled by entities built from point-valued probability functions. The behaviour of those entities is itself determined by the behaviour of functions out of which they are built. Christensen infers from this fact that point-valued probabilistic norms are basic to the epistemology of thick confidence. But that is a faulty projection. Thick confidence is not itself built from credence, and its norms do not derive from those for credence. The metaphysical source of the large-scale properties of our model of thick confidence does not itself model the metaphysical source of the large-scale properties of thick confidence. This is true if the best model of thick confidence is built from entities which model credence. It is true even if that is not so. The point holds no matter how thick confidence is best modelled.

Probabilism captures a slice of a larger epistemic pie. The epistemology of coarse belief captures another slice of the pie. Its focus is on the rational role of a particular thick confidence, namely, the one stretching from the belief-making threshold to certainty. There are

Scott Sturgeon

basic norms for coarse belief; but all basic norms traffic solely in confidence.[8]

References

Christensen, David (2004) *Putting Logic in Its Place*. Oxford, Oxford University Press.

Jeffrey, Richard (1970) "Dracula Meets Wolfman: Acceptance vs. Partial Belief", in *Induction, Acceptance & Rational Belief*, (ed.) Marshall Swain. Reidel.

Joyce, James (2005) "How Degrees of Belief Reflect Evidence", *Philosophical Perspectives*.

Stalnaker, Robert (1984) *Inquiry*. MIT.

Sturgeon, Scott (*forthcominga*), "Reason and the Grain of Belief". Noûs.

———— (*forthcomingb*), *Epistemic Norms*. Oxford, Oxford University Press.

---

[8] It seems fairly likely that all static norms for thick confidence will have limit-case instances modelled by facts about point-valued probability functions. It seems totally unclear whether the same will be true of dynamical norms for thick confidence, whether they will likewise have limit-case instances modelled by standard update rules for probability functions. It seems totally unclear, for instance, that anything like conditionalisation will turn out to be a limit-case instance of a dynamical norm for thick confidence. And this very much calls into question the idea that a full-dress theory of thick confidence will be a generalisation of Probabilism. The topics relevant here go well beyond the scope of this paper. See Sturgeon *forthcomingb*: ch. 6 and 7 for further discussion.

What is Knowledge?

QUASSIM CASSAM

1.

What would a good answer to this question – call it (WK) – look like? What I'm going to call the standard analytic approach (SA) says that:

(A)   The way to answer WK is to analyse the concept of knowledge.

(B)   To analyse the concept of knowledge is to come up with non-circular necessary and sufficient conditions for someone to know that something is the case.

Is the standard analytic approach to WK the right approach? If not, what would be a better way of doing things? These are the questions I'm going to tackle here. I want to look at some criticisms of SA and consider the prospects for a different, non-standard analytic approach (NA) to WK.

Here is one objection to SA: the concept of knowledge can't be analysed, at least if analysis is understood in the way that (B) understands it.[1] (B) assumes a reductive conception of analysis, according to which analysing a concept is a matter of breaking it down into more basic concepts. Let's say that a concept C_1 is more basic than another concept C_2 just if one can grasp C_1 without grasping C_2 but one can't grasp C_2 without grasping C_1. Proponents of SA tend to assume that concepts like *truth*, *belief*, and *justification* are in this sense more basic than the concept *knows* and that that is why they can be used to specify non-circular necessary and sufficient conditions for knowing. If it turns out that such conditions can't be given, and therefore that the concept of knowledge can't be analysed, the net result of combining (A) and (B) will be to make WK unanswerable. If this question is one that we are capable of answering then there must be some other way of answering it.

This objection to SA raises the following questions:

---

[1]   See Williamson 2000: 27–33 for a defence of the view that the concept of knowledge can't be analysed into more basic concepts.

doi:10.1017/S1358246109000010   ©The Royal Institute of Philosophy and the contributors 2009
Royal Institute of Philosophy Supplement **64** 2009

Quassim Cassam

(1) Is it true that the concept of knowledge can't be reductively analysed?

(2) How should WK be tackled if not by giving a reductive analysis of the concept of knowledge?

The first of these questions will be the focus of part 2. I will focus, in particular, on some of Williamson's arguments for what I am going to call the *Unanalysability Hypothesis* (UH), the hypothesis that the concept of knowledge can't analysed in more basic terms. I'm going to suggest that these arguments are less than conclusive.

(2) is worth asking even if one isn't convinced that the answer to (1) is 'yes'. It might be that the concept of knowledge can be reductively analysed but that analysing it in this way isn't the best way of tackling WK. I will consider this possibility in part 3. The upshot is that there are different reasons for rejecting (A). One might do so because one thinks that it requires us to do something that can't be done or simply because one is convinced that there are better ways of tackling WK. The alternative approach that I want to consider – NA – is still broadly 'analytic' in its orientation. It agrees that the key to answering WK is to analyse the concept of knowledge but doesn't think of conceptual analysis in the way that SA thinks of it. So it rejects (B).[2]

What would it be to analyse a concept if not to come up with non-circular necessary and sufficient conditions for its application? The usual answer to this question is that the aim of an analysis should be to provide us with a reflective understanding of a concept, and that the way to achieve that is to *elucidate* the concept rather than, in the traditional sense, to give an analysis of it.[3] So what is it to elucidate a concept? One idea is that it is matter of tracing links between it and other concepts that need not be any more basic. This is how Strawson sees things in this passage:

> Let us imagine... the model of an elaborate network, a system, of connected items, concepts, such that the function of each item, each concept, could... be properly understood only by grasping its connections with the others, its place in the system – perhaps better still, the picture of a set of interlocking systems of such a kind. If this becomes our model, then there will be no reason to

---

[2] There are also non-analytic, naturalistic alternatives to SA that argue that we should focus directly on 'knowledge itself' (Kornblith 2002: 1) rather than on the concept of knowledge but I won't be looking at such views here.

[3] As Williamson remarks, it doesn't follow from the fact that the concept *knows* cannot be analysed into more basic concepts that 'no reflective understanding of it is possible' (2000: 33).

be worried if, in the process of tracing connections from one point to another of the network, we find ourselves returning to, or passing through, our starting-point. We might find, for example, that we could not fully elucidate the concept of knowledge without reference to the concept of sense perception; and that we could not explain all the features of the concept of sense perception without reference to the concept of knowledge. But this might be an unworrying and unsurprising fact (1992: 19).

What Strawson is setting out in this passage is a picture of *non-reductive* conceptual analysis. And one way of understanding NA is to understand it as endorsing (A) with the proviso that analysis is understood along Strawsonian lines rather than along the lines of (B).

The problem with all this talk of non-reductive conceptual analysis, of the project of elucidating the concept the concept of knowledge, is that it is vague and metaphorical. It's all very well talking about the project of tracing connections between concepts but what does this mean in practice? What is the precise nature of the links that the non-reductive story describes and what are the results of elucidating the concept of knowledge? In other words, what is the actual answer to WK that Strawson is proposing? We have the suggestion that the concepts of knowledge and of sense perception are closely related but it's not clear in what sense this is so and how important it is. We might think, for example, that knowledge and perception are connected because knowledge is what perception gives us but does that cast any light on what knowledge is? And where do other sources of knowledge – testimony, reasoning, etc. – fit into the overall story?

These are some of the questions that I will be addressing in part 4, where I will outline a version of NA that builds on two ideas: one is that elucidating the concept of knowledge is, at least in part, a matter of getting a grip on the notion of a *way of knowing*. The other is that ways of knowing are what we appeal to when we want to explain how someone knows, that is, when we want to answer the question 'How does X know?'. Only some answers to questions of this form are good answers. NA says that understanding what counts as a good answer is the key to understanding what knowledge fundamentally is. Perception is important in this connection because of the efficacy of perceptual explanations of much of our knowledge of the world around us. But before spelling out these thoughts let's focus on SA and, in particular, on the response to SA that says that the concept of knowledge can't be analysed.

2.

In *Knowledge and its Limits*, Williamson defends UH. If he succeeds in making it plausible that 'the concept *knows* cannot be analysed into more basic concepts' (33) then SA is in trouble.[4] Analysing the concept of knowledge into more basic concepts can't be the best way of tackling WK if the concept of knowledge can't be analysed into more basic concepts. But how good are Williamson's arguments in support of UH? There are three arguments that we need to consider. The first is what I am going to call the Distinct Concepts Argument (DCA). This argument assumes that every standard analysis of the concept of knowledge *equates* it with a conjunctive concept like *justified true belief*. The aim of DCA is then to show that every standard analysis of *knows* is 'incorrect as a claim of concept identity, for the analysing concept is distinct from the concept to be analysed' (34). Then there is the Inductive Argument. This says that 'experience confirms inductively... that no analysis of the concept *knows* of the standard kind is correct' (30). Finally, there is the False Expectations Argument. The point here is that one should not expect the concept *knows* to have a non-trivial analysis in more basic terms. Few concepts have such analyses, and there is no special reason to expect *knows* to be one of them.

Is DCA any good? This argument relies on the notion of a *mental concept*, so let's start by briefly considering this notion. Although Williamson doesn't attempt a formal definition, he does say at one point that the concept *true* is not mental because 'it makes no reference to a subject' (30). So a concept won't count as mental unless it refers to a subject. This is obviously a long way from constituting a definition of the notion of a mental concept, but Williamson's idea is presumably that we have an intuitive grasp of what mental concepts are, and that this is enough for the purposes of DCA. Now consider the case of a concept C which is the conjunction of the concepts $C_1, \ldots, C_n$. Williamson's proposal is that 'C is mental if and only if each C_i is mental' (29). On this account, *believes truly* is not a mental concept of a state since *true* isn't a mental concept. By the same token, *has a justified true belief* is not a mental concept. These concepts are not mental because they have 'irredundant non-mental constituents, in particular the concept *true*' (30).

Having accepted that *believes truly* and *has a justified true belief* aren't mental concepts, let's also accept, at least for the sake of

---

[4]   All references in this form are to page numbers in Williamson 2000.

argument, that *knows* is a mental concept. What follows from this? What follows is that the concept *knows* can't be the same concept as the concept *believes truly* or the concept *has a justified true belief*. The point is that if C is a mental concept and D is not a mental concept, then they can't be the same concept. But, as Williamson sees things, every standard analysis of the concept of knowledge takes it that this concept *is* the very same concept as some conjunctive concept like *has a justified true belief*. So every standard analysis of the concept *knows* is incorrect.

Crucially, it doesn't matter for the purposes of this argument which particular conjunctive concept the concept of knowledge is equated with, as long as it has the concept *true* as a constituent. For example, suppose that instead of equating the concept of knowledge with the concept *has a justified true belief* one equates it with the concept *has a reliably caused true belief*. Williamson's argument would still go through since 'it applies to any of the concepts with which the concept *knows* is equated by conjunctive analyses of the standard kind' (30). As long as the analysing concept is not mental, it can't be the same as the concept being analysed, and this is the crux of DCA.

Here, then, is a breakdown of the main components of the Distinct Concepts Argument:

(a) Every standard analysis of the concept *knows* equates it with some conjunctive concept which has the concept *true* as a non-redundant constituent.

(b) The concept *true* is not a mental concept.

(c) Any concept with a non-redundant non-mental constituent is not a mental concept.

(d) So the conjunctive concepts with which the concept *knows* is equated by analyses of the standard kind are not mental concepts.

(e) The concept *knows* is a mental concept.

(f) A mental concept can't be the very same concept as a non-mental concept.

(g) So the mental concept *knows* can't be the same concept as any of the conjunctive concepts with which it is equated by standard analyses.

(h) So every standard analysis of the concept *knows* is incorrect.

To get a sense of what might be wrong with DCA consider the following parallel line of reasoning: let us say that a marital status concept is one that says something about an individual's marital status. So, for example, *married, single, bachelor, separated* and *divorced* are all marital status concepts. Where C is the conjunction of the concepts $C_1, \ldots, C_n$, let us stipulate that C is a marital status concept if and only if each Ci is a marital status concept. On this account, *unmarried man* isn't a marital status concept, since *man* isn't a marital status concept. Bachelor is a marital status concept. So *bachelor* and *unmarried man* can't be the same concept.

Something has clearly gone wrong here, because *bachelor* and *unmarried man* are identical if any concepts are. The point is this: the sense in which *unmarried man* isn't a marital status concept is that it isn't what might be called a *pure* marital status concept. It isn't a pure marital status concept because one of its constituents, the concept *man*, isn't a marital status concept. To put it another way, to describe someone as an unmarried man is to say something about his sex as well as his marital status. But if this is why *unmarried man* isn't a marital status concept, then *bachelor* isn't a marital status concept either; to describe someone as a bachelor is, after all, also to say something about his sex as well as his marital status. So there is no longer any basis for the claim that *bachelor* and *unmarried man* can't be the same concept.

This is where the parallel with DCA breaks down. Williamson thinks that *knows* and *has a justified true belief* can't be the same concept because *knows* is a *purely* mental concept whereas concepts like *has a justified true belief* aren't 'purely mental' (30). On this reading of DCA both (d) and (e) need to be slightly modified. Premise (d) should be read as claiming that the conjunctive concepts with which *knows* is equated by standard analyses aren't purely mental because they have at least one non-mental constituent. In contrast, (e) now needs to be read as the claim that the concept *knows* is purely mental. The argument still goes through but is only as compelling as the case for accepting this version of (e).

What is the argument for (e)? Williamson's primary concern isn't to defend the thesis that the *concept* of knowledge is mental or purely mental. His main claim is that *knowing* is a state of mind. This is a metaphysical rather than a conceptual thesis, and he doesn't argue for the metaphysical thesis from first principles. He thinks that 'our initial presumption should be that knowing is a mental state' (22), and then tries to disarm a range of arguments against this presumption. He also concedes that it doesn't follow from the fact that knowing is a mental state that the concept *knows* is mental in his sense. He nevertheless argues that someone who concedes that knowing is a mental state ought to concede that the concept *knows* is mental, that is, purely mental.

Let's call the presumption that knowing is a mental state Williamson's Presumption (WP). Strictly speaking, WP is not just the presumption that knowing is a state of mind. It is the presumption that it is 'merely a state of mind' (21), that is, that 'there is a mental state being in which is necessary *and sufficient* for knowing p'. Presumably, it is only because *knowing* is 'merely' a state of mind that the *concept* of knowing can plausibly be regarded as 'purely' mental. So everything depends on whether we should accept the existence of an initial presumption to the effect that knowing is merely mental.

Williamson claims that 'prior to philosophical theory-building, we learn the concept of the mental by examples' (22). Our paradigms include not just mental states such as pleasure and pain but also non-factive propositional attitudes such as believing and desiring, that is, attitudes that one can have to falsehoods. In contrast, knowing is factive since one can only know that p if p is true. So how is it that factive propositional attitudes are mental given that they are different from non-factive attitudes and also from mental states which aren't attitudes at all? Williamson's answer is that 'factive attitudes have so many similarities to non-factive attitudes that we should expect them to constitute mental states too' (22). Indeed, he maintains that there are *no* pre-theoretical grounds for omitting factive prop-ositional attitudes from the list of paradigmatic mental states. It 'is built into the natural understanding of the procedure by which the concept of the mental is acquired' (22) that the mental includes knowing and other factive attitudes.

What are the similarities between factive and non-factive attitudes? If attitudes are states of mind, then factive and non-factive attitudes are states of mind. But this is not enough for Williamson's purposes. He needs to show that knowing is sufficiently similar to believing and other non-factive attitudes to sustain the presumption that knowing is *merely* a state of mind. This is where the idea that knowing is factive might appear to be in conflict with the idea that it is merely a state of mind. As Williamson's own discussion illustrates, it takes a good deal of sophisticated argument to weaken the prejudice that a factive atti-tude can't be merely a state of mind, and this is difficult to reconcile with the suggestion that we have a pre-theoretical commitment to the idea that knowing is merely mental. Perhaps we don't have a pre-theoretical commitment either way, the concept of the 'merely mental' being a philosophical construct rather than an everyday notion.

There is also a question about the suggestion that WP is built into the procedure by which the concept of the mental is acquired. The procedure that Williamson has in mind is that of learning the concept of the mental by examples, but is this procedure sufficiently well-defined to sustain the suggestion that WP is built into it? Prior to theory-building, what we acquire by example are concepts of particular types of mental state rather than the concept of the mental as such. It's arguable that the procedures by means of which we acquire the concept of the mental leave it open whether knowing is mental in the bland sense that there is a mental state being in which is merely necessary for knowing or in the 'unexpected' (21) sense that there is a mental state being in which is necessary and sufficient for knowing. To acquire the concept of the mental as such is to abstract from the differences between different types of mental state, and this already involves taking on theoretical commitments which might properly be described as 'philosophical'. If this is right, then it is doubtful whether we have any conception of the mental as such, prior to some philosophical theory-building.

This is not an argument for the falsity of (e). It is an argument for the view that (e) hasn't been shown to be true. And that's not the only thing that is wrong with DCA. Its first premise is also dubious: it is false that standard analyses of the concept of knowledge *equate* it with some conjunctive concept that has the concept *true* as a non-redundant constituent. Indeed, it's hard to think of anyone in the tradition that Williamson is discussing for whom concept-identity has really been an issue. The crucial question for SA isn't whether the concept *knows* and, say, the concept *has a justified true belief* are *identical* but whether having a justified true belief that A is necessary and sufficient for knowing that A. One can think that a given conjunctive concept provides necessary and sufficient conditions for knowing without thinking that that concept is 'identical' with the concept *knows*, whatever that means.

The best way of showing that a given concept can be analysed is to analyse it. Ever since Gettier refuted the justified-true-belief analysis of knowledge in 1963 philosophers have been trying to come up with a better analysis. The problem, according to Williamson, is that each successive analysis has been overturned by new counterexamples. This is the basis of the Inductive Argument for UH. This argument claims that UH is confirmed inductively by the long history of failed attempts to provide correct necessary and sufficient conditions for knowing. There are two things that SA can say in reply to this. The first is that fifty years isn't a long time in philosophy, certainly not long enough to justify Williamson's pessimism about the prospects for a reductive analysis of the concept of knowledge. The second is that it needs to be argued and not just assumed that every existing analysis is a failure. Since it is obviously unreasonable to expect anyone to demonstrate the inadequacy of every analysis that has ever been proposed it's tempting to look for a feature that all currently available analyses have in common and that would justify a blanket rejection of them. This is where DCA comes into its own. It purports to identify just such a feature: the presence of the concept *true* in the *analysandum* of that every existing analysis of the concept of knowledge. But DCA doesn't work so it can't be used to justify the premise of the Inductive Argument. Indeed, if DCA or any other such relatively *a priori* argument for UH were successful then the Inductive Argument would be superfluous.

That leaves the False Expectations Argument, which says that there is no special reason to expect a reductive analysis of *knows*. Given that truth and belief are necessary for knowledge, 'we might expect to reach a necessary and sufficient condition by adding whatever knowing has which believing truly may lack' (32). This expectation is based on a fallacy, Williamson claims. For example, 'although being coloured is a necessary but insufficient condition for being red, we cannot state a necessary and sufficient condition for being red by conjoining being coloured with other properties specified without reference to red. Neither the equation 'Red = coloured + X' nor the equation 'Knowledge = true belief + X' need have a non-circular solution' (3).

One question about this argument is whether the analogy with *red* is appropriate. Since Locke introduced the distinction between simple and complex ideas and insisted that simple ideas can't be broken down those who have gone in for reductive conceptual analyses have been careful to argue that only complex concepts are analysable. From this perspective *red* is the paradigm of a simple concept. Its unanalysability should therefore come as no surprise but it doesn't follow that the concept *knows* can't be analysed. More cautiously, it does not follow that this concept can't be analysed if it is complex rather than simple. If *knows* is simple, or if there isn't a viable simple/complex distinction, then the False Expectations Argument goes through. Yet Williamson doesn't establish the simplicity of *knows* or the unsustainability of the distinction between simple and complex concepts. As things stand, therefore, the False Expectations Argument is as inconclusive as all his other arguments for UH.

None of this is to say that the concept of knowledge can be given a reductive analysis. The question is whether it has been *shown* that it can't be, and hence that the answer to (1) is 'yes'. Perhaps there are better arguments against SA than the ones that Williamson gives but the discussion so far suggests that SA is still in the running. In that case, perhaps it would be better for critics of SA to change the focus of their attack. Instead of pressing the point that the concept *knows* can't be analysed, and that SA is a non-starter for this reason, a different line of attack would be to concentrate on whether giving a reductive analysis of the concept of knowledge is the best way of tackling WK even if, as I have been arguing, the possibility of such an analysis hasn't been ruled out. This is the point of (2), and it is to this question that I now turn.

3.

WK is an example of what might be called a 'what' question, a question of the form 'what is X?'. There are many such questions that are of interest both to philosophers and to non-philosophers. Is there anything useful that can be said, in general terms, about the best way of dealing with such questions? Perhaps not, given their sheer variety. But maybe it would help to fix ideas to compare WK with another 'what' question that looks as though it is at least in the same ball park as WK, namely, 'what is depression?' (WD). Though not everyone will agree that WD is in the same ball park as WK the comparison doesn't look completely absurd, especially if one is sympathetic to the idea that knowing is a state of mind. In any case, just to get a sense of the different ways of dealing with a 'what' question let's consider how one might go about tackling WD.

What would a good response to WD look like? People who ask this question are generally interested in such things as the incidence, symptoms, and causes of depression. These are the issues that a helpful answer to WD might therefore be expected to address. One might also expect a good answer to WD to mention the different types of depression and the range of possible treatments. What one would not expect is an analysis of the concept of depression in more basic terms, a statement of non-circular necessary and sufficient conditions for being depressed. Even if the concept of depression can be analysed it just doesn't look as though an analysis is especially relevant if the aim is to say something helpful in response to WD.

This is not to deny that for practical purposes clinicians need something like a definition of depression or at least criteria for diagnosing it.[5] Yet the standard definition – the one given in the American

---

[5]   Thanks to John Forrester for pressing this point and for drawing my attention to the *Diagnostic and Statistical Manual of Mental Disorders*.

Psychiatric Association's *Diagnostic and Statistical Manual of Mental Disorders* – doesn't provide non-circular necessary and sufficient conditions for depression. Instead, it provides two lists of symptoms and stipulates that a patient with major depression must experience at least five of the nine symptoms just about every day for at least two weeks. The emphasis is on necessary conditions rather than necessary and sufficient conditions, and the "definition" is circular: one of the key criteria for major depression is that the patient is in a persistent depressed mood.

How does this help with WK? At the very least it helps by showing that there are questions of the form 'what is X?' that don't call for an analysis of the concept of an X. Saying that a question of this form doesn't call for an analysis of a concept of an X is different from saying that this concept can't be analysed. I haven't said that the concept of depression can't be analysed, only that it *needn't* be analysed for the purposes of answering WD and that the standard clinical definition of depression doesn't in fact amount to a reductive analysis. This suggests that there is at least nothing wrong in principle with the idea that WK doesn't call for a reductive analysis of the concept of knowledge even if such an analysis hasn't been shown to be impossible.

It is true that defenders of SA are unlikely to be impressed by any of this. There are at least three things they can say in defence of their approach:

i. The analogy between WK and WD is no good because WD is not usually understood as a philosophical question. When WK is read in the way that philosophers tend to read it the challenge is not just to say what knowledge is but to say what it is in a special way. This is what Michael Williams is getting at in his comment that 'when we ask "What is knowledge?" philosophically, we mean "Don't just tell us ancillary facts about knowledge: tell us what it is essentially"'(2001, 13). It is when WK is asked in this spirit that it calls for an analysis of the concept of knowledge. In contrast, much of what is usually said in response to WD consists in the specification of ancillary facts.

ii. If the concept of knowledge can't be analysed then it's fair enough that one should be looking for a different approach to WK. But what if we can find non-circular necessary and sufficient conditions for knowing? Wouldn't this be the best possible response to WK? How could a different response possibly be any better? So critics of SA had better concentrate on showing that the concept of knowledge can't be analysed. There is no future in the idea that there are better ways of dealing with WK if the concept of knowledge can be analysed.

iii.   What, exactly, is the alternative to reductive conceptual analysis in relation to WK? At least when it comes to WD we have some idea of what the alternative looks like. Crudely, we can say what depression is by specifying its functional role, its inputs and outputs, causes and symptoms. Can WK be given a functional response? If so, what would a functional account of knowledge look like?

These are some of the challenges to which I now want to respond on behalf of NA. Taking them in reverse order, the aim will be to develop a non-reductive response to WK, to show how it can be at least as illuminating as any reductive response, and to rebut the charge that the non-reductive alternative to SA only succeeds in telling us ancillary facts about knowledge. The non-reductive approach to WK that I want to flesh out has what might be thought of as a broadly functional orientation but parallels with the functional response to WD shouldn't be exaggerated. The key isn't the *function* of knowledge but the *explanation* of knowledge. The proposal is that we can elucidate the concept of knowledge in something like Strawson's sense, and thereby work towards an answer to WK, by looking at what it takes to explain how someone knows, that is, to answer the question 'How does S know?'. The significance of this question for WK might not be immediately apparent but it will hopefully become clearer below.

4.

In his paper "Other Minds", Austin remarks that when we make an assertion such as 'There is a goldfinch in the garden' or 'He is angry' we imply that we know it. Hence:

> On making such an assertion... we are directly exposed to questions such as (1) 'Do you *know* there is?' 'Do you *know* he is?' and (2) '*How* do you know?' If in answer to the first question we reply 'Yes', we may be asked the second question, and even the first question alone is commonly taken as an invitation to state not merely *whether* but also *how* we know (1979: 77).

It is no accident that such questions are normally appropriate. It is something like a conceptual truth that someone who says or implies that he knows that P is exposed to the question 'How do you know?', and this is something that any serious attempt to elucidate the concept of knowledge had better take into account.[6] Perhaps 'I am in pain' is not exposed to this question but such assertions raise special questions that I don't want to go into here.[7]

Here are three issues that now need to be addressed:

(α)   Can one still count as knowing that P if one doesn't know how one knows that P?

(β)   What would count as a satisfactory answer to the question 'How do you know?'

(γ)   What light does any of this cast on WK?

On (α), it's true that people sometimes say 'I don't know how I know; I just know'. We allow that the knower might not know the answer to 'How do you know that P?' but it is much harder to accept that there doesn't have to *be* an answer, known or unknown. Even our willingness to tolerate cases in which the knower doesn't know how he knows has limits. In the primary sense of 'knows' the knower must know how he knows even if he might have trouble articulating his second-order knowledge.[8]

Why does it seem so compelling that when someone knows that P there must be an answer to the question 'How does he know that P?'. The thought is that if someone knows then there must be something in virtue of which he knows. That can then form the basis of a satisfactory response to 'How does he know?'. For example, if the concept of knowledge can be analysed – say as justified true belief – then it might be tempting to say that someone who knows that P does so in virtue of having a justified true belief that P. But, apart from worries about whether the concept of knowledge can be analysed, it's also worth pointing out that 'by having a justified true belief that P' would not normally be taken to be a good answer to 'How does he know that P?'. The reason is that it doesn't *explain* how he knows even if (setting aside Gettier complications) it entails that he knows. This brings us to (β).

Suppose, to take another one of Austin's examples, I assert that there is a bittern at the bottom of the garden and am asked how I know. One answer would be 'I can see it'. Another answer would be 'I can hear it'. Seeing that there is a bittern at the bottom of the

---

6   Cf. Williamson 2000: 252–3.

7   See Hampshire 1979 for further discussion.

8   Compare the account of 'primary knowledge' given in Ayers 1991: 139–44.

garden or, if one prefers, simply seeing a bittern at the bottom of the garden is a way of knowing that there is a bittern there. In general, Φ-ing that P is a way of knowing that P just if it is possible satisfactorily to explain how S knows that P by pointing out that S Φs that P.[9] On this *explanatory* account of ways of knowing seeing that P is clearly a way of knowing that P. Saying that I can see a bittern at the bottom of the garden can explain how I know that there is one there. Someone might question whether I see what I think I see but once it's agreed that I see a bittern then nothing further needs to be done to explain my knowledge of its presence.

Ways of knowing needn't be perceptual. I can know that P by reading that P or by being told that P. Further, as Austin points out, questions of the form 'How does S know?' don't always elicit answers of the form 'S Φs'. 'From its booming noise' and 'I was brought up in the fens' might be given as answers to 'How do you know there is a bittern in the garden?'. Strictly speaking, however, the question to which the former is a response is 'How can you tell it's a bittern?', while the question to which 'I was brought up in the fens' is a response is 'How do you know about bitterns?'. Neither is a satisfactory answer to 'How do you know here and now that there is a bittern at the bottom of the garden?'. Being brought up is the fens is not a way of knowing that there is a bittern at the bottom of the garden; it can't be said that I was brought up in the fens and *thereby* know that there is a bittern there.

Let's agree, then, that a satisfactory response to 'How do you know?' will need to identify one's way of knowing and that ways of knowing are usually expressed by sentences of the form 'S Φs' (where 'Φ' stands for a verb). There are some further points about ways of knowing that are worth making:

I. Ways of knowing needn't be propositional attitudes. I can know that there is a bittern at the bottom of the garden by seeing it but this kind of seeing isn't propositional.

II. For Φ-ing that P to explain one's knowledge that P it is neither necessary nor sufficient that 'S Φs that P' entails 'S know that P'. Not sufficient: 'S regrets that P' entails 'S knows that P' but saying that S regrets that P doesn't explain how S knows; regretting that P isn't a way of

---

[9] See Cassam 2007 for a defence of this approach to ways of knowing. There are parallels between my explanatory conception of a way of knowing and Goldman's conception of an intellectual virtue. There is more on this below.

knowing that P.[10] Not necessary: 'S read that P' can be a good answer to 'How does S know that P?' despite not entailing that S knows that P.

III.   Most ways of knowing are ways of coming to know.[11] Seeing that P, hearing that P, reading that P are all ways of coming to know that P. A possible exception is remembering that P. How do I know that I went on safari last year? I remember. Remembering going on safari is a way of knowing that I went on safari but we might be reluctant to describe it as a way of *coming* to know that I went on safari.

There is an obvious question that is raised by the discussion so far: given the sheer variety of ways of knowing, of acceptable responses to 'How do you know?', what is their unifying principle? What do they all have in common that makes them ways of knowing? The idea that what ways of knowing that P have in common is that they all entail that one knows that P has already been ruled out so where do we go from here? One possibility is that there is nothing further to be said. In practice we have no trouble distinguishing between acceptable and unacceptable answers to 'How do you know?' but no further explanation can be given as to why we accept the explanations that we accept and reject the ones that we reject. There are good and bad explanations of a person's knowledge but our explanations cannot themselves be explained; they have no deeper rationale or unifying principle. I will call someone who argues in this way a *minimalist*.

Minimalism is hard to swallow. As we have seen, acceptable answers to 'How do you know that P?' include 'I perceive that P' and 'I read that P'. Unacceptable answers include 'I guessed that P' and 'I imagine that P'. Is it really plausible that there is *nothing* further to be said about why perceiving that P is a way of knowing that P whereas guessing that P is not? It's surely not irrelevant, for example, that we regard perception as reliable, as delivering a high ratio of true beliefs, whereas there is no temptation to suppose that the same is true of imagination.[12] I will come back to this. In the meantime, there is another proposal to consider. This is the proposal that 'by Φ-ing' is an acceptable answer to 'How does X know that P?' only if Φ-ing is a way of *coming to* know that P. It might seem that this has already been ruled out by the safari example but that's not quite

---

[10]   Unger is someone who thinks that 'S regrets that P' entails 'S knows that P'. See Unger 1975: 158.

[11]   Barry Stroud is an example of someone who treats ways of knowing as ways of coming to know. See Stroud 2000: 3.

[12]   Cf. Goldman 1992.

right. The discussion of that example assumed that 'by remembering' can be a good answer to 'How do you know that P?' and that remembering that P is not a way of coming to know that P. Each of these assumptions might be questioned. Perhaps it is never correct to say 'I remember' in response to 'How do you know?'. Alternatively, one might argue that it is sometimes correct to say this but only because remembering that P *can* be a way of coming to know that P.

In what sense can remembering that P be a way of coming to know that P? Suppose that P is the proposition 'I am now on safari'. What is true is that I do not come to know that I am now on safari by remembering that I am. But what if P is 'I was on safari'? In that case, I can come to know that P by remembering that I was. Memory, like testimony, is the source of one's knowledge of many propositions of the form 'I was F', just as perception is the source of one's knowledge of many propositions of the form 'I am F'. Perception, memory and testimony are all capable of *yielding* knowledge of the appropriate propositions, and that is why seeing that P, remembering that P and reading that P all count as ways of knowing that P.

This brings us, finally, to (γ): what light does the explanatory account of ways of knowing cast on WK? Here is one suggestion: once we have an idea of the sorts of things that can yield the knowledge that P we can then proceed to give an account on this basis of what it is to know that P. In effect, this will be an account of knowing in terms of ways of knowing. Snowdon considers something like this possibility in a discussion of what he sees as the necessary link between knowledge and perception. He says that evidence of such a link 'comes from our treating it as totally unproblematic that someone's knowledge that P can be explained by saying that they saw that P' (1998: 301). This then leads to the suggestion that 'our fundamental understanding of knowledge is as what is yielded by perception in certain circumstances' (ibid.).[13] This is a partly functional response to WK.[14] To say that knowledge is what perception gives us is to give an account of knowledge in terms of its inputs. The account is also non-reductive since it doesn't say that the concept of

[13] This is not Snowdon's own view.

[14] Thanks to Paul Snowdon for suggesting this characterization. A fully functional account would need also to say something about the 'outputs' of knowing. Just as inputs to knowledge are what explain how someone knows, we can think of its outputs in terms of what attributions of knowledge enable us to explain – action, for one. In this way one might hope to say something useful about the value of knowledge. Merely talking about ways of knowing won't enable one to do that.

perception is more basic than that of knowledge. Just as our fundamental understanding of knowledge is terms of its inputs so our fundamental understanding of perception is in terms of its outputs, the key output being knowledge: 'perceiving an object is, in its nature, a way to get knowledge about the object' (Snowdon 1998, 300).

One problem with this response to WK is that it neglects non-perceptual sources of knowledge. However, such sources can easily be accommodated by saying that knowledge is to be understood as that which is yielded by perception, memory, testimony, introspection, calculation, and so on. To put it another way, to know that P is to be in a state that one can get into in any number of different ways, for example, by seeing that P, hearing that P, reading that P, calculating that P, and so on. This is an explanatory conception of knowledge, to go with the explanatory conception of ways of knowing: our fundamental understanding of (propositional) knowledge is that it is something whose possession by an individual can properly be explained by reference to any one of an open-ended list of ways of knowing or, if one prefers, ways of coming to know.[15] Non-circular necessary and sufficient conditions for knowing are not to the point.

We now have a version of NA, that is, a non-standard analytic response to WK. It's an analytic response because it focuses on the concept of knowledge. It's a non-standard analytic response because it doesn't try to give a reductive analysis of the concept of *knows*; instead, it seeks to elucidate this concept by relating it to other concepts that are no more basic. Specifically, it elucidates the concept of knowledge by relating it to the concept of a way of knowing and to concepts of specific ways of knowing. It's hard to see why this non-reductive approach to WK should be seen as less helpful or illuminating than the standard reductive approach or as only telling us ancillary facts about knowledge. It is not an ancillary

---

[15]   The explanatory conception of knowledge builds on the thought that 'a necessary condition of being in some states may be having entered them in specific ways' (Williamson 2000: 41). There are also parallels between the idea that to know that P is to be in a state that one can get into in any number of different ways and Williamson's idea that 'knowing that A is seeing or remembering or. . . that A, if the list is understood as open-ended, and the concept *knows* is not identified with the disjunctive concept' (2000: 34). Seeing and remembering are what Williamson calls 'ways of knowing' but his conception of ways of knowing is different from mine. See Cassam 2007: part 3, for an account of the differences. Notice, finally, that the explanatory conception can allow that perceptual ways of knowing are privileged in relation to some non-perceptual ways of knowing. See Cassam 2007 for further discussion.

fact about the knowledge that P that it can be acquired by seeing that P. Clearly, there are lots of things about the world around us that can't be known in this way but we might still think that perception is a basic source of our knowledge of many empirical propositions. In any case, the present version of NA takes care not to ignore non-perceptual ways of knowing.

The biggest challenge facing this approach to WK is to the suggestion, or implication, that it can do without a reductive analysis of the concept of knowledge and that it therefore has no need for SA. To put it at its most abstract, the worry is that the concept of knowledge is prior to that of a way of knowing and that any attempt to elucidate the former by reference to the latter is doomed. For example, suppose we say that seeing that P is a way of knowing that P whereas wishfully thinking that P is not a way of knowing that P. We might try to explain this difference by saying that only seeing delivers a sufficiently high ratio of true beliefs but why assume that reliability is relevant to ways of knowing? Surely this assumption can only be justified by a prior analysis of the concept of knowledge along reliabilist lines. If, as simple reliabilism says, knowledge is true belief caused by a reliable process then it is not hard to figure out why wishfully thinking that P isn't a way of knowing that P. But if simple reliabilism is correct then it already provides a standard analytic response to WK without reference to ways of knowing. So it seems that NA collapses into SA.

There are several things that are wrong with this line of argument. To start with, it is false that a reliability condition on knowledge can only be justified on the basis of a reductive analysis of the concept *knows*. From the fact that reliability is necessary for knowledge it doesn't follow that a reductive analysis of the concept of knowledge is possible.[16] It is also debatable whether we can explain why seeing counts a way of knowing solely in terms of reliability. Imagine that I form beliefs about what is going on in distant parts on the world on the basis of what my crystal ball tells me and that my crystal ball is as reliable as ordinary seeing. On a particular occasion I assert that the American President is in Iowa. My answer to 'How do you know?' is 'I can see in my crystal ball that he is in Iowa'. Is this an acceptable answer? If not, then seeing in my crystal ball that P is not a way of knowing that P. Yet seeing (in the ordinary sense) that P is a way of knowing that P. Since (*ex hypothesi*) there is no difference in reliability between ordinary seeing and crystal ball gazing it can't be maintained that it is sufficient for ordinary seeing

[16]   Cf. Williamson 2000: 100.

to be a way of knowing that it delivers a high ratio of true beliefs; one can imagine crystal ball gazing or clairvoyance doing that.

In that case, what does explain the fact that seeing is a way of knowing? To answer this question we can borrow some insights from virtue epistemology. Virtue epistemologists like Goldman try to give an account of the nature of justified belief. Their idea is that a justified belief is one that is obtained through the exercise of intellectual virtues but they do not propose a definition of intellectual virtue. Instead, Goldman 'posits a set of examples of virtues and vices as opposed to a mere abstract characterization' (1992: 158). Exemplary intellectual virtues include 'belief formation based on sight, hearing, memory, reasoning in certain "approved" ways, and so forth' (ibid.). Why do these count as intellectual virtues? Reliability is one factor but it is also important that they are ways of obtaining *knowledge*; they are belief-forming processes that would be 'accepted as answers to the question "How does X know"'(1992: 162). Novel or unusual belief-forming processes are then evaluated as virtuous as long as they are sufficiently similar to the exemplary virtues.

NA should think of ways of knowing somewhat in the way that Goldman thinks of intellectual virtues. They are ways of obtaining knowledge and they wouldn't count as ways of obtaining knowledge if they didn't deliver a high ratio of true beliefs. But in figuring out what counts as a way of knowing we don't start with a blank slate and then work up to a list of ways of knowing on the basis of considerations like reliability. The position is rather that we start with a list of exemplary ways of knowing, exemplary responses to "How does X know?" such as perceiving, and work up from there to the identification of further ways of knowing and ultimately to a more abstract characterization of the notion of a way of knowing.[17] On this account, the status of exemplary ways of knowing such as perceiving is not something that can be explained in more basic terms. If our *fundamental* understanding of knowledge is as what perception gives us then there is no question of perceiving that P failing to be a way of knowing that P.[18] And if this sounds like a sophisticated form of

---

[17]   It may well turn out on this account that seeing in one's crystal ball that P is a way of knowing that P. It all depends on whether this kind of seeing is sufficiently similar to ordinary seeing. Sufficient similarity will include phenomenological similarity.

[18]   Even sceptics should accept the link between perceiving and knowing. They should concentrate on the issue of whether it is ever possible for us to see that P, where 'P' is a proposition about non-psychological reality.

minimalism then so be it. When it comes to explaining why certain explanations of our knowledge are good ones there is only so far we can go.[19]

University of Warwick

References

Austin, J. L. (1979) "Other Minds", in *Philosophical Papers*, 3rd Edition. Oxford, Oxford University Press.

Ayers, M. R. (1991) *Locke*. London, Routledge.

Cassam, Q. (2007) "Ways of Knowing", *Proceedings of the Aristotelian Society*, **CVII**.

Goldman, A. (1992) "Epistemic Folkways and Scientific Epistemology", in *Liaisons: Philosophy Meets the Cognitive and Social Sciences*. Cambridge, Mass., The MIT Press.

Hampshire, S. (1979) "Some Difficulties in Knowing", in *Philosophy As it Is*. (eds.) T. Honderich and M. Burnyeat. Harmondsworth, Penguin.

Kornblith, H. (2002) *Knowledge and its Place in Nature*. Oxford, Oxford University Press, 2002.

Snowdon, P. F. (1998) "Strawson on the Concept of Perception", in *The Philosophy of P. F. Strawson*. (ed.) L. Hahn. Chicago and Lasalle, Open Court.

Strawson, P. F. (1992) *Analysis and Metaphysics: An Introduction to Philosophy*. Oxford, Oxford University Press.

Stroud, B. (2000) "Scepticism and the Possibility of Knowledge", in *Understanding Human Knowledge*. Oxford, Oxford University Press.

Unger, P. (1975) *Ignorance: A Case for Scepticism*. Oxford, Clarendon Press.

Williams, M. (2001) *Problems of Knowledge: A Critical Introduction to Epistemology*. Oxford, Oxford University Press.

Williamson, T. (2000) *Knowledge and Its Limits*. Oxford, Oxford University Press.

[19] Thanks to Ciara Fairley and Paul Snowdon for comments on an earlier draft of this paper. Thanks also to audiences at the Royal Institute of Philosophy and the Cambridge University Department of History and Philosophy of Science.

The Value of Knowledge and The Test of Time

MIRANDA FRICKER

The 'Problem'

The fast growing literature on the value of knowledge stems from a compelling Pre-theoretical Intuition: Knowledge is more valuable than mere true belief. This Pre-theoretical Intuition gives rise to the Value Question: What makes knowledge more valuable than mere true belief? And that question, finding no immediate answer, gives rise to the Value Problem: The problem we can seem to have in answering the Value Question. Our primary difficulty in answering the Value Question is that when we look at any standard example of a mere true belief, and compare its value with the value of the correlative knowledge state, it is not immediately clear that knowing p *is* any more valuable than merely truly believing p. Let's rehearse a standard sort of example. You wake up in the night to the loud bleeping of the smoke alarm. You form the belief that there's a fire; so you immediately get everyone out safe and dial 999. As it happens, your belief is true, for there is a fire in the basement; but the smoke alarm is faulty and went off at random. You have a true belief, but lack knowledge. So what? What greater value would a state of knowledge have been? You got everyone out and dialled 999. The value bestowed on a mere true belief by the fact that it is true seems to exhaust the value of the counterpart knowledge. Here we confront the Value Problem.

It all started with *Meno*. Socrates and Meno have been discussing whether a person's being good is a matter of knowledge or not, and Socrates is proposing that being good, and being able to show others the right path, might rather be a matter of true opinion:

> **Socrates:** Look – suppose someone *knew* the way to Larissa (or wherever) and was on his way there, and showing other people how to get there; obviously he'd be good at showing them the right way?
> **Meno:** Of course.
> **Socrates:** And what about someone who had an *opinion* on how to get there – a correct opinion – but who'd never actually been there, and didn't know how to get there; wouldn't he be able to show them the way as well?

doi:10.1017/S1358246109000034

Meno: Of course.

Socrates: ...With his true belief, but without knowledge, he'll be just as good a guide as the man with the knowledge? [Meno agrees.]...

Socrates: So in other words, a correct opinion does just as much good as knowledge?

This last question inspires some fleeting resistance from Meno, but soon gives rise to Meno's famous question about the value of knowledge, a question which has inspired much of the recent literature.

Meno: Except in one respect, Socrates. If you have knowledge, then you'll *always* be dead on target; but if you only have a correct opinion, sometimes you'll hit, and sometimes you'll miss.

Socrates: What makes you say that? If you've always got the correct opinion, won't you always be 'on target' as long as you've got your correct opinion?

Meno: Yes, good point...it seems that must be right; which leaves me wondering, Socrates: If that's the case, why on earth is knowledge so much more valuable than correct opinion, and why are they treated as two different things?[1]

The way Meno puts it, in his conjunctive question at the end here, suggests that whatever makes knowledge more valuable than correct opinion is the same thing that crucially differentiates the two. Some version of this idea is surely right, but I shall argue that the particular way in which the idea is played out in the literature helps to distort the debate, and effectively conceals at least one of the most fundamental aspects of the value of knowledge. My principle aims here will be to identify two key presumptions that together effect the distortion and concealment; and to give a positive account of what I take to be one of the most basic values of knowledge – a value that Socrates points to in the answer he goes on to give to Meno's question, but which can only be missed or misconstrued within the confines of much of the current debate.

The Diagnosis: Two Unwarranted Presumptions

In the literature we see the value problem crystallizing into a highly specific shape. And the contributions are partisan in terms of the

---

[1]   Plato 2005: 129.

general epistemological team that the contributor is on. The value problem seems to present itself to most who tackle it as a challenge and an opportunity to advance whatever particular epistemological theory they espouse. Indeed, the value problem – very distant now from its origination in Meno's epistemologically innocent value question – has become something of a modern epistemological football. This has two disadvantages: any proposed solution is hostage to epistemological fortune in that it stands or falls along with the particular analysis of knowledge that issues it; and it encourages players to look for the value of knowledge in something that distinguishes their theory of knowledge from their competitors' theories, when in fact the basic value of knowledge may be better explained by reference to something less epistemologically specific. Spectators to the literature have seen a movement away from the most basic reliabilist line, and a surge in the general direction of credit accounts of one or another stripe. Given how the ground-rules of the game have developed, credit accounts come to seem admirably well kitted out to solve the problem. They are; but I believe that the way the ground-rules have developed distorts the natural philosophical question, so that we have ended up with a somewhat artificial game. In order to explain what I mean, I shall describe the general trajectory of the literature, and then give my diagnosis of the pressures that give it the peculiar shape it now has.

There is a range of different credit accounts, but the common idea is that what gives knowledge its special value is the credit that is transferred to the knowledge state from the agent for achieving his true belief in the manner requisite for knowledge. Quite what that manner is depends on the particular stripe of the credit account. (On John Greco's agent reliabilist view, for instance, the subject's true belief must be due to some stable trait of cognitive character; on Ernest Sosa's view, the true belief must be 'attributable' to the knower as his own doing; and Duncan Pritchard argues, in this volume, in favour of an agent reliabilism supplemented by a safety condition.[2]) At the virtue epistemological end of the spectrum is the view, advanced by Linda Zagzebski, that the agent's credit worthiness is a matter of her good epistemic motive, most fundamentally, her love of truth. I shall focus on Zabzebski's account[3] because

[2]   See, in particular, John Greco 2002; Ernest Sosa 2002; and Duncan Pritchard, 'Knowledge and Value', this volume.
[3]   I shall focus in particular on Zagzebski 2003; but see also her earlier paper, which makes similar negative arguments against forms of reliabilism, though is less worked out in terms of her own position: Zagzebski 2000.

it provides a good illustration of both how satisfying an account of the value problem can be within the framework of the current debate, while simultaneously exposing the features of that framework that I want to highlight and reveal as unduly limiting the range of answers we might give to the value question.

She sets up the issue by considering and rejecting reliabilist responses to the value question. Reliabilism says that a true belief arrived at by a reliable process or faculty is more valuable than a true belief arrived at in any other way, and that added value is the value of knowledge. But, argues Zagzebski, this answer does not work, because reliability is only as valuable (or disvaluable) as that which it produces. Reliability *per se* has no value. She invokes an example to bring the point home: a great espresso made from a reliable espresso machine is no more valuable than one made from an unreliable machine. A great espresso is a great espresso; a true belief is a true belief. This argument is justly challenged by Pritchard[4], who points out that it assumes there are only two kinds of value – intrinsic and instrumental – whereas in fact there is a third category of value, sometimes called 'final' value. If something has final value, we value it to that extent for its own sake (and so non-instrumentally) but not in virtue of its intrinsic properties. Whereas intrinsic value is possessed in virtue of intrinsic properties, and instrumental value accrues in virtue of what something is a means to, final value is possessed in virtue of other relational properties. Granted that reliability in itself has no value, still the reliabilist could claim that a true belief reliably produced is valuable for its own sake in virtue of certain relational properties. In the case of agent reliabilism, for instance, the relational property in question might be that of being produced by a stable trait of intellectual character. Certainly that looks like a plausible claim of value, and it is one not catered for by Zagzebski's line of attack. Given the existence of final value as a species of value, then, Zagzebski is not entitled to assume that reliability's lack of intrinsic value means it is impossible that some kind of reliability in how true beliefs are generated could constitute the value of knowledge; for the value of knowledge might yet turn out to be owing to relational properties associated with epistemic reliability. But I will not dwell on this, as my main purpose lies elsewhere.

In Zagzebski's discussion, having dispensed with reliabilism, she goes on to press the positive case for her virtue epistemological solution

[4]   Duncan Pritchard, 'Knowledge and Value'. For related criticisms, see also Philip Percival's response to Zagzebski, Percival 2003.

to the value problem. Seized by the question how a component of knowledge can *transfer* value to the knowledge state itself, she pursues the idea that just as, in general, good motives add value to the acts that they produce, so do good epistemic motives add value to the acts of belief that they produce. A true belief motivated by a good epistemic motive thus acquires the added value of the good motive: and that's the special value of knowledge. But, she observes, there can of course be cases where the true belief achieved is in itself not worth having, for the content of a true belief might be trivial, or in various ways bad. Illustrating trivial true belief, she invokes Sosa's example: 'At the beach on a lazy summer afternoon, we might scoop up a handful of sand and carefully count the grains...' (Sosa, 2003: 156).[5] Illustrating bad true beliefs, she mentions 'knowing exactly what the surgeon is doing to my leg when he is removing a skin cancer; knowing the neighbour's private life'.[6] Still, argues Zagzebski, in all such cases, the agent gains a certain credit for the good epistemic motive that led her to acquire the belief, and so that which renders her true belief knowledge is *admirable*. This admirability is to be distinguished from *desirability*, which is a matter of the content of one's cognitive state being worth having (not trivial or worse than trivial). Not all knowledge is desirable; but all knowledge is admirable. A particularly valuable kind of knowledge concerns true beliefs that are both desirable and admirable – knowledge worth having; and the best kind of knowledge (a 'great good'[7]) is when not only the admirability but also the desirability of the true belief can be credited to the agent – knowledge acquired by the agent because it is worth having.

Given the way the issue shapes up, Zagzebski's proposed solution to the value problem presents itself as a satisfyingly subtle and differentiated proposal, albeit dependent on one's accepting a virtue-based analysis of knowledge. But I think there is a deep problem associated with her approach to the value question, and which is a generic problem with credit accounts. In short, they put the cart before the horse. Credit accounts purport to explain the fact that we value knowledge by pointing to the value of this or that form of epistemic creditworthiness – on Zagzebski's view the credit that transfers in all cases of knowledge to render it admirable (even where the content fails to render it desirable) is owing to the good epistemic motive that helps transform true belief into knowledge. But the idea that we value knowledge *because* we value good epistemic

[5] Ernest Sosa 2003: 156.
[6] Zagzebski 2003: 21.
[7] *Ibid*. 24.

motive gets the order of explanation back to front. We do not value knowledge because we value good epistemic motive. Rather, we value good epistemic motive because we value the knowledge it tends to get us. Indeed such a motive only constitutes a good epistemic motive because it aims at knowledge or truth or some other suitably ultimate epistemic end. (The general point can be made equally well in terms of true belief rather than knowledge: we value good epistemic motive because of the truth it tends to get us. Either way, the point is that the value of good epistemic motive is most naturally to be explained by reference to the value of what it gets us, and not the other way around.) So to suggest that we most fundamentally value knowledge because we value good epistemic motives, or whatever else is suggested as earning the relevant credit, is to put the cart before the horse.

The natural order of explanation marks a point of disanalogy between virtue epistemology and virtue ethics. In virtue ethics, it is a thoroughly plausible idea that the value of the various goods that virtues aim at cannot be specified independently from the values of the good motives animating the virtues. It is entirely plausible to say there is a non-vicious circularity in how we characterize these values – the virtuous agent is motivated towards the good, and the good cannot be specified independently from what motivates the virtuous person. But this becomes, at best, a far less plausible idea when transferred to the field of epistemological value. For it is all too easy to specify the value of truth, and thereby the knowledge that captures it for us, in purely practical terms without reference to our epistemic motives: we need plenty of true beliefs in order to successfully pursue our practical and other purposes in life. (We don't need *all* our beliefs to be true, of course; there are exceptions. We can generally afford to have a few false beliefs knocking around without any real consequence; in some circumstances, we might be pragmatically better served by some false simplifications of the truth; and sometimes we might personally need a fairly substantial false belief in order to be able to face another day. But the basic point stands.) Approached from this angle, the value problem presents itself as the question what good it does us to possess true beliefs specifically *as* knowledge, and so the question of knowledge's value now seems more adverbial: what is the greater value of possessing truths in the manner of knowledge?

I think an adverbial formulation captures the right way to approach the issue, but advocates of credit accounts do not naturally approach it in that way because they are committed to identifying the value of knowledge in something that does not reduce to the value of truth.

That is one of the purported lessons of the critique of the reliabilist solution to the value problem: 'If the feature that converts true belief into knowledge is good just because of its conduciveness to truth, we are left without an explanation of why knowing p is better than merely truly believing p.'[8] This can seem to flow from the critique of reliabilism, but even disregarding the reservations about that critique to which Pritchard's objection gives rise, the lesson really only flows given a certain unwarranted presumption about how to frame the value question. The credit approach, and the value problem literature quite generally, is characterized by an unwarranted *Synchronic Presumption*, according to which the value question is conceived as a question about the comparative values of mere true belief and knowledge at a snapshot in time. At best, we are invited to compare a mere true belief that p and knowledge that p in a very short time frame. Accordingly, we tend to concentrate on what is of value in one or another moment's cognitive grasp of the directions to Larissa, rather than what epistemic transformations might occur as one trudges along the road, meeting other people along the way, passing or not passing various landmarks one had expected, and so on. Now, the Synchronic Presumption confines our philosophical attention to the present, and this has consequences for the lesson that Zagzebski draws from her critique of reliabilism – that the value of knowledge must be 'truth-independent'. The presumption causes a conflation of two quite different requirements of 'truth-independence', one narrow and one broad: (a) the narrow requirement that the value of knowledge be independent of the value that its constituent true belief already has in virtue of being true; and (b) the broad requirement that the value of knowledge be independent from the value of truth quite generally. It is a crucial motivation for credit accounts that the requirement of truth-independence is taken as the broad one in (b), for if the requirement were merely narrow as in (a), there would be far less motivation to cast the philosophical eye inward into the character of the agent in order to find some element, in itself supposedly independent of the value of truth, which contributes the distinctive value of knowledge. The Synchronic Presumption helps construct the value problem to suit certain styles of 'solution'.[9]

---

[8] Zagzebski 2003: 17.

[9] We see this phenomenon in more obvious form in the so-called tertiary value problem – the 'problem' of revealing the value of knowledge as *different in kind* from the value of truth (or from the value of whatever else may fall short of knowledge – see the definition given in Pritchard, this volume). The tertiary value problem really is a piece of philosophical

The conflation of (a) and (b) obscures the possibility that the value of knowledge (or one fundamental value of knowledge) *is* in fact reducible to the value of truth, even while remaining independent from the value of the truth of the constituent true belief. Thus it conceals the possibility that the value of knowledge consists in something about knowledge that helps us retain our true beliefs over time. Pursuing the way(s) in which knowing assists our general purchase on truth is, I think, the right way to approach the value question. The answer Socrates gives to Meno's question points us in this direction.

The Superior Resilience of Knowledge

The conclusion given in the *Meno* about the value problem is that knowledge is more valuable than true opinion because it is 'shackled'. Like the statues of Daedalus which were so life-like that people tied them down to stop them running away, states of knowledge are shackled so that we do not lose them. Now it is explicit in Plato's text that the metaphor of 'shackled' (or 'tethered') is intended by Socrates to signify awareness of reasons or evidence for the belief:

> **Socrates:** If you own an original Daedalus, unshackled, it's not worth all that much – like a slave who keeps running away – because it doesn't stay put. But if you've got one that's shackled, it's very valuable. Because they're really lovely pieces of work. What am I getting at? My point is, it's the same with true opinions. True opinions, as long as they stay put, are a fine thing and do us a whole lot of good. Only, they tend not to stay put for very long. They're always scampering away from a person's soul. So they're not very valuable until you shackle them by figuring out what makes them true... And then, once they're shackled, they turn into knowledge, and become stable and fixed. So that's why knowledge is a more valuable thing than correct opinion, and that's how knowledge differs form a correct opinion: by a shackle'.[10]

If this is on the right track, and I think it is, then the value of knowledge will only reveal itself once we abandon the synchronic

---

artifice, corresponding to no natural philosophical intuition or question. It has surely come into being largely for the benefit of those with a 'solution' at the ready.

[10]   Plato 2005: 130.

conception of the issue for a *diachronic* one. We have to conceive of epistemic subjects as placed in time in order to reveal the crucial difference: mere true beliefs are typically more vulnerable to being lost in the face of misleading counter-evidence. Reconsider the road to Larissa – and I shall try to be as epistemologically non-partisan as possible, assuming only what Socrates rightly assumes in his comment above, that knowledge typically involves arriving at one's true belief on the basis of some suitable evidence or reasoning. The extra value in knowing the route as opposed to merely having a true opinion is that, over time, one is likely to come up against counter-evidence (you chat to a passer-by who says it's the other way, you see a signpost that pranksters have turned to point the wrong way) and if you have some grasp of the evidence for your belief, as you typically will if you have knowledge, then you are in a better position to weight the new evidence. You are therefore less likely to abandon your true belief for a false one in the face of misleading evidence. The point is, possessing a true belief in the manner typical of knowledge shrinks the class of counter-evidence one will be misled by.

We want to possess truths because we need them to serve all our various purposes, but considered diachronically this entails that we value possessing them in a manner that is conducive to our retaining them over time in the face of misleading counter-evidence. Now one can instantly imagine various epistemically undesirable ways of doing this: sheer dogmatism will lead one to hold on to one's beliefs, including true ones, in the face of any counter-evidence, including misleading counter-evidence. But, given our diachronic perspective, it is clear that dogmatism is epistemically undesirable because it is a thoroughly indiscriminate strategy over time. Sheer longevity is not what the value of knowledge consists in. Rather, I suggest we take Plato's prompt that the value of knowledge resides in a tendency to survive the test of time in virtue of some kind of rational advantage. I suggest we coin a notion of 'resilience'. Resilience is: *the tendency to survive misleading counter-evidence owing to the subject's being in a position to weight it against positive evidence already possessed.*

Resilience names a typical feature of knowledge, not a necessary condition. It follows from the minimal assumption that knowers typically have a suitable grip on reasons in favour of their belief, and that although this is not necessary for knowledge, it is none the less a central distinctive characteristic. Socrates explicitly has this characteristic in mind, for he says that mere true opinions are 'not very valuable until you shackle them *by figuring out what makes them true...* And then, once they're shackled, they turn into knowledge, and become stable and fixed'. Although Socrates' comments are often interpreted as advocating a tripartite analysis of knowledge as justified true belief, there is no real commitment to any such thing taken as crucially distinct from most alternative modern analyses. It is historically more plausible to see modern analyses as variations, of a theoretically complex and highly inter-reactive sort, on the broad generalization rehearsed by Socrates, to the effect that knowing things typically involves believing them truly for a reason. This non-specific and minimal assumption about what typically distinguishes knowledge leaves my proposal non-partisan with respect to what might provide an adequate analysis of knowledge, and indeed to the question whether there could be any adequate analysis of knowledge.

Also taking his cue from the *Meno*, Tim Williamson has briefly made a similar suggestion in the context of his case for knowledge's being a prime condition, and as such unanalysable. The context of his discussion is of course epistemologically partisan in its anti-analytical commitment, though I think something like his point can be made in the non-partisan spirit I am urging for responses to the value question. Williamson is not primarily engaged in establishing any particular answer to the value question as such, but rather in establishing the superiority of knowledge construed as a prime condition when it comes to predicting and explaining action. In the course of that framing argument, however, he draws the crucial conclusion about the value of knowledge, that 'present knowledge is less vulnerable than mere present true belief to *rational* undermining by future evidence', and that is indeed the point we should draw out of Socrates's remarks.[11] However, his argument for this proceeds exclusively on the basis of two rather specific sorts of comparative case. Firstly, the case in which mere true belief is lost upon discovery that it was based on a false belief, whereas knowledge cannot be lost in that way because a true belief arrived at by way of a false lemma is not knowledge. And, secondly, the case in which mere true belief is lost upon discovery of misleading counter-evidence abundant in one's environment, whereas knowledge cannot be lost in that way because a true belief possessed in a context in which it might be defeated at any moment by counter-evidence is too unstable to constitute knowledge.

That Williamson relies so specifically on these two sorts of case to establish his conclusion, with which I agree, however renders his argument peculiarly vulnerable to the invocation of mirror

---

[11]   Williamson 2000: 79.

image examples of circumstances in which knowledge is more readily lost than mere true belief. Jonathan Kvanvig has exploited this strategy to argue against Williamson, specifically constructing examples to mirror the case where there is misleading evidence in the environment. Kvanvig's examples illustrate how the advent of such evidence can cause one to lose precisely not true belief, but knowledge. For instance, he suggests that one's mathematical knowledge could be lost owing to a renowned mathematician's mistakenly asserting (in a suitably public domain, yet unbeknownst to one) something to undermine it. An example like this aims to remind us that our knowledge can come and go without our awareness, and so knowledge in general might come to seem just as elusive in the face of counter-evidence as is true belief. In similar vein, we could perhaps construct an example to mirror the false lemma case: A visitor to the U.K. forms the true belief that Gordon Brown is a powerful figure in British politics on the basis that Gordon Brown is Chancellor of the Exchequer. But then when (shortly after the visitor has left, and unbeknownst to her) Gordon Brown stops being Chancellor to become Prime Minister, her knowledge is lost – yet her true belief remains. Whatever one makes of such cases, I think the moral here is that if one makes the case for knowledge's greater rational persistence too much by way of specific cases, the argument risks descending into a competition over how many examples can be lined up on either side to influence our sense of what is rule and what is exception.

After giving his mirror examples to the misleading evidence scenario, Kvanvig concludes that Williamson's claim that knowledge displays superior rational persistence is at best contingently true. He regards this as an objection, evidently assuming that if knowledge does have a distinctive value, then that value will apply to all possible cases of knowledge without exception. He emphasizes his objection by pointing out that one could be at a possible world in which most of our beliefs are fixed not by evidence at all, but rather pragmatically, in which case most of our true beliefs would not be knowledge but would be none the less robustly persistent in the face of misleading counter-evidence. (Of course, like dogmatically held beliefs, they might persist in the face of *any* counter-evidence, but Williamson would not be able to dismiss the pragmatic scenario by pointing to the fact that our beliefs would simply not be in 'good order', for they would be in good order pragmatically speaking.) Maybe so, but we should reject Kvanvig's assumption that revealing the contingency of Williamson's thesis amounts to an objection. On the

131

contrary, Williamson's anti-analytical epistemological position means he is explicitly committed to its being impossible to define knowledge, as distinct from mere true belief, in terms of knowledge's greater rational persistence, and it follows that there will be exceptions to the rule that knowledge has greater rational persistence. For present purposes I aim to remain non-partisan on the question of the analysis of knowledge, but there is in any case simply no reason to expect a solution to the value problem to amount to an exceptionless claim about knowledge; it should be obvious to us from the start that it may simply be a generalization. (I shall return to this shortly.)

Accordingly, the resilience proposal wears its admission of exceptions on its sleeve. It is explicitly only a generalization to say that knowledge typically involves possession of evidence so that knowers are at an advantage when it comes to weighing in new counter-evidence. Clearly, we can allow that there are circumstances in which knowledge would lack resilience, or where its resilience would lack its usual value. For we can allow that there are exceptional circumstances in which knowledge is possessed without the usual evidential awareness, and exceptional circumstances in which retaining one's true belief beyond the snapshot in time is simply of no interest. In such circumstances, we may readily admit, the knowledge in question would indeed lack the value it more normally possesses. Similarly, the resilience proposal also wears its more general contingency on its sleeve. It is manifestly a generalization confined to worlds significantly like this one. These worlds are, I take it, worlds in which most of our beliefs are fixed not pragmatically but more by evidence (even if some of them are partly *formed* as the result of pragmatic pressures, they none the less stand susceptible to evidential defeaters); and in which, most of the time, we achieve our true beliefs not by way of false lemmas and not in contexts where we are either already surrounded by soon-to-be-observed existing misleading evidence, or soon-to-be-introduced-into-the-environment misleading evidence. These sound like exceptions to the rule and they surely are.

The cases on which Williamson so specifically bases his own argument, however, can help substantiate our more generally motivated resilience version of Socrates' point. They remind us that when we possess mere true beliefs, we may do so not only by complete fluke (as in my opening standard example of the true belief that there is a fire in the house – such happy flukes must almost never happen), but more often with some grip on the evidence, where that grip is inadequate – perhaps because it is flawed by a false lemma, or because it is rendered insufficiently stable by not-yet-observed mislead-ing evidence. This supports the claim that it is typical of knowledge, as opposed to mere true belief, that one is in a better position to weigh in new counter-evidence, and so one is less likely to be misled. It is not that in most cases of mere true belief we have no grasp whatever of the evi-dential situation, but rather that, given we are falling short of knowl-edge, our grasp is bound to be inferior with respect to that crucial task of weighing new counter-evidence with existing evidence.

The value of resilience is of course reducible to the value of truth taken generally, for it is wholly derived from the value of sustaining true beliefs over time. But the resilience of knowledge is none the less a value over and above the value of the truth of any constituent true belief, which is the only value of truth made visible on the Synchronic Presumption at work in the value problem literature. The value of any item of knowledge is therefore not truth-independent in the broad sense given in (b); but it is indepen-dent from the pre-existing value of the truth of the constituent true belief, as is required in (a). By restricting our attention to the present, and so conflating (a) and (b), the Synchronic Presumption conceals the possibility that the value of knowledge consists, at least in part, in its superior resilience.

I said it should be obvious to us from the start that an account of the value of knowledge might take the form of a generalization about knowledge rather than a necessary condition. But we saw that Kvanvig presumes that Williamson must be aiming for a claim of neces-sity, and in this presumption he is in the good company of most contri-butors to the value problem literature, not least because most are in the business of advocating their preferred analysis.[12] Why should it come as such a shock to entertain a thesis about the value of knowledge that is not a thesis about all possible cases of knowledge? The answer lies in a second presumption distorting the debate and limiting the responses we might make to the value problem: let us call it the *Analytical Presumption*. This is the presumption that the distinctive value of knowledge must be ready-contained in whatever warrant is said to convert mere true belief into knowledge. This methodological pre-sumption stems from the analytical enterprise in epistemology, and whatever one may think about the wisdom of that enterprise vis-à-vis achieving an enlightening philosophical characterization of knowledge,

---

[12]   Needless to say there is absolutely nothing wrong in principle with advocating one's preferred position on any philosophical issue. My point is diagnostic, and only critical in so far as the partisanship has helped distort the value question.

it has certainly had a distorting effect on the present debate. The Analytical Presumption partly explains the attractiveness of credit accounts, for they locate the value of knowledge precisely in the allegedly ready-made form of the agent's epistemic credit that principally plays the warranting role. The Analytical Presumption is therefore a driving force behind the unfortunate cart-before-the-horse strategy of locating the value of knowledge in something whose own value can only be explained by reference to the prior value of ultimate epistemic ends such as knowledge. As I say, credit accounts can give satisfying solutions to the value problem as we have come to recognize it. But what we have come to recognize as the value problem has been substantially misshapen by the twin pressures of the Synchronic Presumption and the Analytical Presumption. The first presumption rules out the reducibility of the value of knowledge to the value of truth, and conceals the significance of the test of time; the second insists that the value of knowledge is to be found in some kind of warrant, and so conceals the possibility that a good response to the value question might be a generalization about what is distinctive of knowledge, and not a purported necessary condition.

A Different Diagnosis

Jason Baehr too has argued that the literature on the value of knowledge is, as it stands, on the wrong track.[13] He observes that the literature is premised on the idea that there is a powerful and widespread pre-theoretical intuition to the effect that knowledge is more valuable than mere true belief, and he calls this the 'guiding intuition'. He rightly observes that the guiding intuition is treated in the literature as placing a constraint on the analysis of knowledge, in the sense that any viable analysis must entail that knowledge is indeed more valuable than mere true belief. And he argues that the guiding intuition is not in good shape. Firstly, it would have to express an exceptionless generalization about knowledge; yet it is implausible that we have a real pre-theoretical intuition that expresses any such thing. Secondly, he argues it would have to be 'formal'; that is, the guiding intuition would have to have no specific content beyond the fairly empty idea that knowledge is more valuable than mere true belief. It would have to be 'formal' in this sense, in order to make sense of the fact that there are so many contender vindications of it in the literature.

---

[13]   Jason Baehr *forthcoming*.

The Value of Knowledge and The Test of Time

As my own arguments here make manifest, I am in complete agreement with the first point, that for the guiding intuition to provide a proper motivation for the literature as we know it, the intuition would have to be exceptionless, and that this is implausible. Baehr invokes the chief counter-examples of trivial knowledge and immoral knowledge. Recall Sosa's example of counting the grains of sand. If we bother to do so, we may well achieve knowledge, but a piece of knowledge that clearly has no greater value than a trivial mere true belief with the same content. Such a triviality is not worth knowing any more than it is worth believing. Then, at the other end of the scale, there is immoral knowledge, such as knowledge of how to stir up ethnic hatred, or instigate genocide. Knowledge of these things has no greater value than the counterpart mere true beliefs, for they are so horrible that, again, such things are not worth knowing any more than they are worth believing. And so, argues Baehr (and contrary to Zagzebski, who, as we have seen claims admirability even for undesirable knowledge), knowledge is not *always* more valuable than truebelief; and the guiding intuition is false. Thus one of the two chief motivations for the value problem literature as we know it – the guiding intuition *qua* strict universal – collapses. Agreed. Of course, one could always find ways of plausibly presenting our pre-theoretical intuition as in itself exceptionless. For instance, I think it is plausible to present it in a refined version that rules out the exceptions above, as expressing the idea: If there's value in believing it, then there's more value in knowing it. (An epistemic analogue to the proverb, 'If a job's worth doing, it's worth doing well'.) But this indeterminacy in how precisely to express our pre-theoretical intuition only serves to support Baehr's point, since our refined version would not provide a proper motivation for the literature as we know it. That literature aims to find the value of knowledge somewhere in a set of necessary and sufficient conditions for knowledge, and it follows that its guiding intuition must be an intuition about all cases of knowledge.

My point of disagreement comes only with the second argument: that the guiding intuition would have to be 'formal', that is, contentless beyond the mere claim that knowledge is more valuable than mere true belief. The thought here is that in order to motivate the array of philosophical appropriations of the guiding intuition, that intuition would have to say nothing substantive about why we value knowledge; yet it is implausible that we have any such empty pre-theoretical intuition. So the guiding intuition is found,

Miranda Fricker

on this score too, to be false. While I appreciate the argumentative aim here, I do not see that the guiding intuition would have to have no content beyond the sheer idea that knowledge is more valuable than mere true belief. It is commonplace for pre-theoretical intuitions of all sorts in philosophy to be in need of unpacking and/or clarifying. The puzzle of identifying what is implicit in a given intuition – and sometimes this can be the same thing as identifying its basic grounds – is just the sort of thing that different philosophical theories compete to solve. And I see no reason to regard the value of knowledge literature as straying from this standard model. While I can agree it is implausible that we have a pre-theoretical intuition which contains not even an inkling of why knowledge is more valuable than mere true belief, still it seems to me entirely plausible to say we have a pre-theoretical intuition whose inkling of substantive content is implicit, or confused, or in some other way ready for philosophical explicitation and development. In this respect, it seems to me, the guiding intuition stands.

While I agree, then, with Baehr's conclusion that there is something profoundly amiss in the value of knowledge literature, I prefer a different diagnosis. My diagnosis points to the significance of two presumptions: the Synchronic Presumption, which obscures the twin possibilities that the value of knowledge is reducible to the value of truth, and that it is to be revealed in knowledge's advantage in surviving a certain test of time; and the Analytical Presumption, which misleads us into thinking the value of knowledge must come ready-made in some kind of warrant, and, therefore, into thinking that if there is a positive answer to be found to the value question, then it must apply to all possible cases of knowledge. Both presumptions serve to obscure the fundamental value of knowledge, which, taking my cue from Plato's Socrates, I have been arguing for in terms of knowledge's superior resilience. More broadly, we might say that both presumptions obscure the significance of the test of time, but in slightly different ways. The Synchronic Presumption obscures it simply by confining our attention to the present snapshot in time; and the Analytical Presumption obscures it by directing the philosophical gaze to the retrospective matter of the aetiology of the true belief (was it formed by way of a reliable faculty/agent/good epistemic motive?) and so away from the prospective matter of how well it will survive misleading counter-evidence as time goes by.

No doubt resilience is not the only basic value of knowledge. Another presumption one might explore the extent of in this

136

The Value of Knowledge and The Test of Time

debate is that of individualism. If we expand our conception of the value question not only through time to embrace the diachronic perspective I have been urging but also out across social space, we may find that the only true beliefs that we may responsibly pass on to others by testimony constitute knowledge, and, correlatively, that the only true beliefs we should accept from others constitute knowledge. If so, the two-way sharability of truths is another basic value of knowledge.[14] A key point I hope to have put across is that approaching the question of knowledge's value from an epistemologically partisan point of view has tended to carry unwarranted presumptions into how the issue is viewed, presumptions that actively obscure the value of resilience. While all approaches have their point, and are likely to reveal some layer of knowledge's value – most accounts are after all addressing, in some form or other, the evidential sensitivity that marks out knowers – there is clearly a role for different, and less partisan approaches to this question, so that we may achieve a fuller picture of the different, often interrelated, values of knowledge.[15]

Birkbeck College

---

[14]   Edward Craig's *Knowledge and The State of Nature* can be read as an extended explanation of the value of knowledge in terms of the sharability of truths, though his argument is not geared explicitly to the value question, but rather to a practical explication of why we come, of necessity, to have the concept of knowledge at all. But one instantly sees how such an explication of why we have the concept might simultaneously constitute an explanation of its value. (See Craig 1990). Martin Kusch has discussed Craig's genealogy as providing a social explanation of knowledge's value in Kusch *forthcoming*. Ward Jones's early paper on the value question also places Craig's work and the issue of testimony centre-stage; see Jones 1997: 423–439.
[15]   I presented earlier versions of this talk to a Workshop on the Value of Knowledge at the University of Copenhagen, organized by Klemens Kappel; and at research seminars at the University of Glasgow and University of Bristol. I thank all those who took part for their questions and comments. I am also grateful to Alan Millar for a conversation that first prompted me to latch on to the idea that knowledge's value has something to do with the handling of counter-evidence; and to Jason Baehr for discussion and subsequent email exchanges that helped clarify the differences between our views.

Miranda Fricker

References

Baehr, Jason. (*forthcoming*) "Is There a Value Problem?" in *Epistemic Value*, (eds.) Adrian Haddock, Alan Millar, and Duncan Pritchard. Oxford, Oxford University Press.

Craig, E. (1990) *Knowledge and the State of Nature: An Essay in Conceptual Synthesis*. Oxford, Clarendon Press.

Greco, J. (2002) "Knowledge as Credit for True Belief" in *Intellectual Virtue: Perspectives from Ethics and Epistemology*, (eds.) Michael DePaul and Linda Zagzebski. Oxford, Clarendon Press.

Jones, W. (1997) "Why Do We Value Knowledge?", American Philosophical Quarterly, **34**:**4**, 423–439.

Kusch, M. (*forthcoming*) "Testimony and the Value of Knowledge" in *Epistemic Value*, (eds.) A. Heddock, A. Millar and D. Pritchard. Oxford, Oxford University Press.

Percival, P. (2003) "The Pursuit of Epistemic Good" in *Moral and Epistemic Virtues*, (eds.) Brady and D. Pritchard. Oxford, Blackwell.

Piato. (2005) *Protagoras* and *Meno*, trans. Adam Beresford. London, Penguin.

Pritchard, D. (2009) "Knowledge and Value" in this volume, (ed.) Anthony O'Hear. Cambridge University Press.

Sosa, E. (2002) "The Place of Truth in Epistemology" in *Intellectual Virtue: Perspectives from Ethics and Epistemology*, (eds.) DePaul and Zagzebski. Oxford, Clarendon Press.

Williamson, T. (2000) *Knowledge and Its Limits*. Oxford, Oxford University Press.

Zagzebski, L. (2000) "From Reliabilism to Virtue Epistemology" in *Knowledge, Belief and Character*, (ed.) Guy Axtell. Lanham, Maryland: Rowman and Littlefield.

———— (2003) "The Search for the Source of Epistemic Good" in *Moral and Epistemic Virtues*, (eds.) Brody and Pritchard. Oxford, Blackwell.

Index of Names

Ackerman, Bruce 12–13
Anderson, Alan Ross 46
Austin, J.L. 112, 113
Ayres, Ian 12–13
Baehr, Jason 134–36
Barnes, Barry 4
Bloor, David 4
Boghossian, Paul 4, 5, 6
Byrne, R.M.J. 47, 48
Craig, Edward 137
Christensen, David 89, 96–7, 99
DeRose, Keith 66, 67, 77, 82
Descartes, Rene 1, 65
Dretske, Fred 66, 81, 84
Elgin, Catherine 31
Fleck, Ludwig 2
Foucault, Michel 2
Fuller, Steve 3
Galileo 5
Gettier, Edmund 108
Goldman, Alvin 54, 55, 115, 119

Goodman, Nelson 49, 55
Greco, John 19, 20–3, 27, 123
Hume, David 1
Jackson, Frank 47
Jeffrey, Richard 91–2
Jones, Ward 137
Kaplan, Mark 19
Koppl, Roger 10, 15
Kornblith, H. 102
Kuhn, Thomas 2
Kvanvig, Jonathan 19, 20, 31, 34–7, 131, 133
Lackey, Jennifer 28, 38
Lakatos, Imre 2
Latour, Bruno 2, 4
Lewis, David 47, 48, 55
Locke, John 91, 109
Nozick, Robert 66, 75, 76, 77, 81
Plato (*Meno*) 121–22, 128, 129, 136
Pritchard, Duncan 80, 123, 124, 127
Pryor, James 82–3

Putnam, Hilary 65
Ramsey, Frank 55, 92
Reid, Thomas 1
Riggs, Wayne 31
Rorty, Richard 5
Saks, Michael 10
Sartwell, Crispin 20
Socrates 121–22, 128, 130, 136
Sosa, Ernest 22, 80, 123, 125, 135
Snowdon, Paul 116–17
Stalnaker, Robert 48, 92
Strawson, P.F. 102–103, 112
Stroud, Barry 115
Unger, Peter 115
Williams, Michael 111
Williamson, Timothy 19, 80, 101–109, 117, 130–33
Woolgar, Steve 2
Zagzebski, Linda 19, 22, 31, 32–3, 34, 123–28, 135